Devil Dolphins of Silver Lagoon
and Other Stories

EXPANDED EDITION

110 Koji Nakamura The whole chapter
129 mad driving in the 3rd world
to 131
135 – a not too respectful riff on sport diving as well...sport ?
151 Fairy Tern description – lovely
165 imaginations come undone
169 Melville quote "looked like Yasgur's Farm after Woodstock"
252 The Ship

Capt Michael Bennett

Title ID: 3454653
Title: Devil Dolphins of Silver Lagoon and Other Stories
Subtitle: Adventures of a Reluctant Photographer's Assistant
Description: From the sailing whales in Patagonia to the neurotic attack dolphins of Brazil, a behind-the-scenes view of the making of many of Flip Nicklin's National Geographic Magazine stories.

ISBN1452873925
EAN-139781452873923
Primary Category Travel / Special Interest / Adventure
Country of Publication United States
Language English
Search Keywords humor travel whales
Contributors *Authored by* Capt Michael Bennett
Cover Photographs by Flip Nicklin

Front and back cover photos by Flip Nicklin.

Praise for Devil Dolphins

Midwest Book Review
> *"Nature photography isn't as simple as it seems. Devil Dolphins of Silver Lagoon and Other Stories is a collection of stories as Michael Bennett reflects on what occurs sometimes when these pictures are taken, and while they aren't always pretty, they can prove very amusing. ...an exciting read, not to be missed."*

Kirkus Review
> *"A debut collection that goes beyond ordinary fish tales. Over the course of his maritime career, Bennett has traveled all over the world in a variety of occupations, often as part of a team from National Geographic, affording him a unique perspective that allowed him to witness events from behind the camera and behind the wheel. This book contains elements of solid travel writing, from cultural misunderstandings and local cuisine to harrowing conditions and unexpected detours. A respectable first effort full of entertaining anecdotes."*

San Francisco Book Review
> *"Captain Michael Bennett has been places most of us can only imagine, and along the way, he's had experiences both amazing and baffling. Whether it's being hassled by surly dolphins, befriending a hermit crab on a treacherous island, spearheading the rescue of an orphaned orca, or relying on sheer luck to cross conflict-stricken Sri Lanka, Bennett has plenty of engaging tales to tell. Devil Dolphins of Silver Lagoon and Other Stories is a collection of anecdotes and stories from his travels far and wide, and it's a delightful read."*

Table of Contents

Photos

For the old Sporty, wherever she may be.

Foreword

The idea for writing some of these stories came a couple of years ago when a bunch of us old whale guys had gotten together and were sitting around reminiscing, as usual, around a bottle of wine after dinner (*"Remember when that whale grabbed Flip in Argentina and dragged him around..."*... the rest of us going, *"Yeah, heard that a million times, but that was nothin', what about that time..."*)...that sort of thing. Anyway, it dawned on us that we had done most of the things we were talking about and that it might be interesting for others to hear these stories as well.

For my part I jotted down the following collection as I remembered my version of some of these events. (At this point everybody has their own versions of events, fixed now through constant retelling and possibly some gray matter ossification....)

Most of my stories involve the *National Geographic Magazine* assignments I was on with Flip Nicklin over the past few decades, with a few Maui and shipboard tales thrown in when they seemed relevant.

There is a bit of license here and there, mostly timeline changes and the like, to make the story easier to follow, but, for the most part, this is what happened.... At least how I remember it happening.

The great thing is that we are still doing this stuff. I'm just waiting for Flip to call with the next adventure; I will of course drop everything and go.

Michael Bennett
Seattle
July, 2010

Note for expanded edition:

At the request of some of my friends and well-meaning readers, (they seemed well-meaning anyway...maybe they just didn't believe the stories and wanted proof...), I have added to this expanded edition some pictures plus a couple of additional stories. This has been great fun. I especially liked the book signing/wine-tasting events we did, so I am working on another book so we can do it again.

MB
December, 2016

Devil Dolphins of Silver Lagoon

Brazil Nuts

Pink River Dolphins? The phone message was from my friend Flip Nicklin, but the sound quality was terrible. It sounded like he was talking from the bottom of an empty dumpster. Flip and I had been working together on various watery projects ever since we had met on a whale shoot in Maui some years before and he would call me occasionally when he needed a boat captain or assistant diver on one of his photo adventures. He was calling from some far-flung place or other and it sounded like he was saying that he needed a diving assistant for a *National Geographic* story he was about to do that involved (I had to listen to it again) pink river dolphins in the Amazon. Sure enough, no mistake about it, that's what he said. So upon the second listening I gathered that it was actually the dolphins that were pink, not the river. I had gotten to the point that nothing about these calls from Flip surprised me anymore.

Was I available? Absolutely. I wasn't about to miss something like that. I left a return message telling him to sign me up, then set about clearing my schedule and digging out all of the assorted gear I'd accumulated on previous adventures with Flip; khaki stuff with lots of pockets, and of course the solar-powered pith helmet with its little cooling fan I'd been so fond of on the trip to Sri Lanka. I didn't want to be heading off into the Amazon jungle without the right outfit.

This was all to happen fairly quickly. We had a chance to meet up with some Brazilian dolphin researchers in the interior city of Manaus and visit their floating camp in the Rio Negro, a tributary of the Amazon, where they were studying these pink dolphins. We would be leaving in about a week, pending the *National Geographic* travel department arranging tickets and visas and such, so I took advantage of the time to do a little research.

One of the more interesting bits of information I was able to gather on the *boto* (the local name of the dolphin) went like this: local belief had it that the *boto* shape-shifted at night into a handsome young man who would come ashore, seduce and impregnate the local girls, and then return to the river and reassume dolphin shape at dawn—the ultimate deadbeat dad. It was one of the most convenient and practical legends I'd ever heard, and that explanation would have come in handy in a couple unfortunate situations in my hometown when I was growing up. It turned out that there was also a thriving black market in dried *boto* genitalia, apparently used as an aphrodisiac and probably driven to some degree by that same legend. This sounded like one interesting animal, and I was anxious to see one.

The departure day arrived, Flip and I met up at the Geographic headquarters in DC, gathered up numerous cases and boxes of gear and cash, and we were off.

I was excited to see that we were flying initially to Rio de Janeiro before connecting on to Manaus. It was only a brief stop, but at least I would get to see the place. I had always been fascinated by the stories and reputation surrounding Rio. I remembered being struck by a newspaper article I'd read of the thousands of people hospitalized each year as a result of their Carnival celebration, and I wondered at the time just what a Carnival celebration in Rio entailed. It sounded like quite a party and something everybody should see at least once.

It turned out I wasn't to be introduced to any of the charms of Rio on this trip however, as our flight arrived late and we were unwillingly entered into one of those desperate airline connection sprints, lugging considerable gear across a vast expanse of nightmarishly expanding airport corridors, to a connecting flight that there doesn't seem to be an outside chance of making in time. And usually, sure enough, there isn't. But of course, just our luck, we made this one.

We dashed onto the plane at the last possible moment, and I said goodbye to the lights of Rio as we took off. (At least I think they were the lights of Rio, they may have been the spots of light caused by hyperventilation you see behind your eyeballs just before you pass out.) At any rate we were finally off toward the Amazon.

And things, naturally, went awry almost immediately. These trips seldom followed our proscribed plans once launched, and this time was no exception.

We had both commented on a strange vibration that had started about halfway into the flight and sure enough, about halfway into the flight we were informed that there was some problem with the plane, and that we would be stopping off mid-way at the Brasilia airport for an undetermined time while it was fixed.

This was welcome news to me actually. I had read about Brasilia, this newly-built city that was envisioned first as a saint's prophecy, then as a political concept, and then actually carved out by force of will in the sparsely populated center of the country. The idea was that the former capital, Rio, being located on the coast, was too far from the center of things to be practical in this vast country, so they decided to make a new one. I was more than a little curious to see what it was like.

But it was...odd. Not what I expected. As we broke through the clouds there appeared below what appeared to be the form of a giant butterfly or bird on an immense plateau, like the ancient Nazca line figures in Peru, but perfectly symmetrical. As we got closer, you could make out the structures and streets, with one wide boulevard running down the center, or spine. What a huge undertaking. And construction was going on all around the bird figure, growing away from the planned center. Hundreds of thousands of people had been somehow compelled to make their way here to the center of Brazil where in the recent past there had been no city, no structures, just a scattering of indigenous people...and now there was a teeming metropolis. Incredible. Like creating and manning an outpost on the Moon.

We got on the ground without incident and it was there in the Brasilia airport that I discovered that Portuguese, the language of Brazil, (and with which I have no familiarity), sounds when spoken very much like Spanish (with which I am somewhat familiar), but the familiar sounds are meaningless to a non-Portuguese speaker. The result is a chronic confusion much like that reported by certain head trauma or stroke victims who

4

hear what they know are familiar words and phrases but are incapable of understanding. Imagine:

"*Que? Como?*" I would ask (meaning *What? How?* in Spanish).

"*Que? Como?*" they would echo (meaning *When? Who?* in Portuguese). It went on like this for a time. It was a lot like the old "Who's On First?" Abbott and Costello routine.

So I suspect it was disconcerting to the well-meaning Brazilians at the airport who were engaged in talking to me in Portuguese about the plane troubles as I nodded earnestly along with them, when at the end of the conversation, to our mutual surprise, my sudden blank look indicated a total lack of comprehension. I usually detected a glance of sympathy as they edged quietly away.

Ultimately, though, it was determined that the plane wouldn't be leaving for at least several hours, so we had time to look around a bit. We decided to take a cab ride into the city with no particular destination, just to see what it looked like.

I'm not sure what it was that unnerved me about the place, but it gave me a creepy, vacant feeling. Everything was concrete; buildings, walls, streets, huge concrete modern art structures placed at regular intervals, everything neat and tidy and grey, including the few people we saw outdoors. Almost everyone we saw was in a vehicle, just a handful of pedestrians wandered along the expansive boulevard. I remember thinking that it reminded me of nothing so much as one of those science fiction movies that showed cities of the future where humans were groomed and kept as food sources, and people mysteriously disappeared when they reached a certain age. Very likely an overreaction...I knew we probably weren't going to be eaten, but it was almost a relief to get back to the airport and spend the next few hours perched uncomfortably on a modern-shaped concrete bench waiting for the plane to be fixed before we were allowed to reboard and continue our trip.

Manaus, when we finally got there, turned out to be the opposite in every respect. If Brasilia lacked history and soul, then Manaus overcompensated on both counts.

Oops, there goes... another rubber tree production plant...

Talk about a colorful past. Manaus had been the center of the booming rubber producing industry at the turn of the century, and incredible wealth had poured into the area in a short time. An opulent European style city had sprung into being in the jungle, complete with a world-class opera house and a replica of the famous Parisian marketplace, designed by the Eiffel Tower guy (who, judging by how often you hear about *him*, seems to have designed almost everything in the world around that time period, including our own Statue of Liberty). It must have been an incredible thing to see the city in its heyday, well-dressed Europeans in their carriages on their way to see the latest Italian opera star. Picture Klaus Kinski in *Fitzcarraldo*—the movie was actually filmed there.

However, the boom had gone bust just as quickly as it had arrived when synthetic rubber was developed about twenty years later, and elegant Manaus was left moldering in the jungle. Imagine, at some time in the future, a European city like Budapest decaying in the latter stages of global warming as the tropics have engulfed the higher latitudes, and all of the wealthy people have fled to cooler climes farther north.

And it was indeed hot. On the equator hot. And the Amazon River was a total surprise to me. It was the dry season, so instead of a vast expanse of water filling the jungle as I had imagined, it looked more like the local city reservoir during a terrible drought. A vast expanse of muddy junk-filled bank stretched down to the water, several hundred yards or more on either side of sticky dark mud, with long rows of planks stretching out to makeshift docks floating at the edge of the brown water. The river was still huge though, flowing there in its brown mud valley; ocean going ships were anchored in the middle a thousand miles from the sea. I could only imagine how vast the river was in the wet season when it overflowed its banks.

Our first order of business after we arrived and got settled into our hotel was to check out the famous marketplace. Not only were we anxious to see it, of course, but also were very curious about the tales of *boto* body parts being offered for sale, and we figured the marketplace was as good a place as any to see if the rumors were true. It was easy to find; you could hear and smell it before it actually came into view, a huge sprawling structure on the riverbank. It was thronging with colorful crowds and vendors, fish bins and cooking stalls, clothing and toy sellers, and there was a constant din. We entered through the big wrought-iron front gate into long corridors of stalls selling everything imaginable, and some unimaginable.

If we were going to find dolphin genitals for sale, this was the place. And sure enough, after asking indelicately around for the aphrodisiac department (just imagine yourself asking for *"medicine for strong love"* in a heavy accent at your local marketplace) we were directed to a little stall at the end of a gloomy tunnel where a bright-eyed little gnome sat happily among dangling dried up unrecognizable animal parts and jars of nightmarish floating things.

It turned out there were innumerable aphrodisiac products and theories, more than you might think necessary. There were potions and poultices aplenty…this was one stop shopping for the lust-impaired. We finally located the *boto* section, and the proprietor showed off his wares, but seemed a little put out when it became evident that we didn't actually want to *buy* any of the bits and pieces, just take pictures of them. We probably ended up on some Manaus vice squad watch list. (Keep an eye on *these* guys; I'm not sure what they're up to….) It was obviously time to exit the marketplace. I was starting to imagine we were getting funny looks from virtually everybody.

We surfaced from the stalls into the fierce tropical sun of the city. We'd gotten the alleged *boto* body part pictures we'd gone in there for, but seeing the dried up animal parts didn't convey any sense whatsoever of the animal itself. They could have been selling clumps of dried road kill for all we knew; and, for the *boto*'s sake, we hoped they were.

We weren't scheduled to meet the dolphin research boat until early the next morning, so we spent the rest of the day touring the tarnished splendor of old Manaus, and picking up a few supplies. There were pictures and drawings of the *botos* everywhere, they seemed to be a local icon, much like the killer whales are icons in the Northwest, and I was developing a real curiosity about this dolphin. I couldn't wait to actually see a live one.

Pepto Dismal

Sunrise the next morning found us making our way out along a slippery trail of planks across the mud bank out to a floating dock where the little tender boat waited to transport us out to the research boat, which was anchored a ways up the Rio Negro (Black River), which empties into the Amazon at Manaus. While the water flowing out of the Rio Negro wasn't exactly black, it was definitely dark; you could see the stain of it spreading for miles down the Amazon from where the two rivers joined, and there was a uniform dark color from the mouth all the way up to the anchored boat. We were thinking this didn't bode too well for the underwater animal shots Flip was hoping to get.

The boat itself when it finally came into view looked like something from a Disneyland ride. It was one of those double-decker "hammock boats" that were found along the Manaus waterfront, very picturesque with its wooden hull and white wooden picket railings. They were called "hammock boats" because the entire lower deck was one big sleeping area, just a big space with hooks and posts for hammocks, while the upper deck was the business level, with the pilot house, galley, and cabins set aside in this case for the research team.

The researchers were expecting us, they had quite a setup, the anchored boat stayed put as the home base, while several smaller tenders would go off during the day to various observation stations and return to tie up at night. It was just like similar research groups everywhere, mostly young university kids living on meager rations and happily focused on their work. We were told to stash our stuff in one of the upper cabins and were issued hammocks and told we could stake out our sleeping area wherever we could find a spot on the lower deck.

9

Our getting settled in would have to wait, however, one of the tender boats was preparing to leave, and the crew invited us to come along, so we grabbed some cameras and gear and hopped aboard. Just like that we were off, heading up the Rio Negro in search of the *boto*. I was so anxious to see one of these things, not only were dolphins not supposed to be in fresh water, they certainly weren't supposed to be pink, this was going to be amazing.

We cruised up the brown river, the mud banks stretching above us on either side, and the air began to get noticeably hotter.

Then we saw them. Bright pink objects breaking the dark surface of the river, the backs of the *botos* as they came up for a breath. Their pink color was vivid, the color of Pepto Bismol, just as described. This was almost too easy.

But it was frustrating. All you could make out was the rounded back, a bright splash of color, and only for a second as they grabbed a quick breath and submerged again.

We watched them from the boat for awhile; they seemed to be feeding in one area, so we pulled over to the bank and went ashore to set up our observation camp. (I imagined I was getting some envious looks from the fellow researchers when I produced my sun helmet with its little fan, but the glances may have had some other meaning entirely...it was hard to read.)

They continued to feed out in front of our station, tantalizing glimpses of color above the brown water. We made occasional forays out into the river with the boat to try to collect anything left floating after they surfaced, hoping for bits of whatever they were eating or fecal samples, carefully preserving whatever was found,

Flip snapping away with the camera whenever a shape broke the surface. But the water was like diluted coffee, you could barely see into the stuff.

They stayed in the same area all day and continued teasing us with flashes of pink. But it felt unfulfilling. We were very happy to see them, of course, but we weren't seeing much. I desperately wanted to get a sense of the whole animal and I knew Flip was anxious to get some underwater shots. We exchanged a frustrated glance as the group packed up and we headed back around sundown, the oven-like heat finally abating somewhat. We were hoping conditions would be better tomorrow.

After dinner back aboard the main boat, (rice and fish seem to be universal fare on these projects), we had a chance to visit with the other researchers, sharing stories, getting caught up in their enthusiasm and good humor. Later the group started drifting down below to the sleeping deck, and we decided we'd better follow suit and figure out the arrangement.

We commandeered a couple of likely spots on either side of the space and settled in for the night amid the usual good-natured jibes and insults as the lights went out, just another group of primates going about their nocturnal routine. It was quite the dormitory arrangement.

But when I awoke in the middle of the night and looked around in the moonlight I had a strange moment of disorientation. I imagined I was inside a burrowing insect hive, like a termite colony, with a dozen or so hammocks filled with snoring humans swaying and jiggling in the half-light. I'll never forget it.

The next day was much like the first, lots of surface shots, but impossible to see far into the murky

11

water. We were told that the visibility wasn't likely to get better; it wasn't a function of mud or water level, as we hoped was the case, this was coloring from vegetable matter upstream. So getting any underwater shots here in the near future wasn't a high probability.

The researchers, when they saw what we were up against, had a few recommendations for us if we needed underwater shots, however. It seemed that recently this new-age psychic woman who claimed she was traveling the country communicating with dolphins using crystals had come through the Rio Negro camp. She told the researchers that there were fresh water lakes in the south of the country that had dolphins introduced into them where the visibility was good, and she said that she had just come from there.

That was good enough for us. Armed with that kind of sterling information, we had to check it out; we hadn't had any luck communicating with them using our methods, and we certainly weren't getting any more useful pictures this way, so what the hell.

We got the names and general location of these lakes. The first one had recently had a small, fresh water dolphin called Tucuxi introduced into it as a tourist attraction for a lakeside water park. The other, Lagoa de Prata, or Silver Lagoon, was farther south by the town of Belo Horizante. It reportedly had a couple of *botos* introduced into it to eat the piranhas that were scaring the swimmers at the resort there.

So it was off southward for us. We made our reluctant farewells, turned in our hammocks, returned to Manaus and headed off, following as good a lead as we were likely to get.

A Fresh Assault

The first lake was just as described, a seedy little water park, with rides and water slides going into the lake, and a small marina with paddleboat rentals. But, it was off-season and everything was closed. However, we could see two little dolphins surfacing out on the lake. Amazing. We had to get out there. We found a caretaker wandering around the park and talked him into renting us one of the paddleboats, a treacherous little affair with a bicycle pedal and chain arrangement that turned a tiny paddle at the stern, but it was the only water borne vessel around.

We tossed our gear aboard, the caretaker cast off our lines with a bemused look, and we pedaled and splashed our way out toward where we had seen the little dolphins surface. And this was where things went sideways.

The little dolphins went nuts. When they spotted us churning slowly towards them they made a beeline for our boat, leaping out of the water, obviously excited. And were they ever cute, perfect little specimens, like miniature cartoon bottlenose dolphins you might see at Children's Sea World. This was great. They were coming right for us while Flip snapped away with the camera and I pedaled frantically. And they kept coming, right up to the boat, and actually started rubbing against it, flushed with excitement. We were getting great pictures.

And then it struck us. It had something to do with the deranged look in their eyes as they twitched and rubbed themselves along the side of the boat. Something was wrong here. These little guys were actually humping our boat. It was just wrong.

Imagine meeting some kid you think is a charming sixth-grader whom you discover is really an evil circus dwarf when he suddenly lights up a big stogie and starts hitting on your wife. Unsettling.

Somewhat shaken we extricated ourselves from the area and made our way back to the dock, feeling soiled. These animals had obviously been isolated here too long; they desperately needed freedom, or failing that, therapy.

Possibly in need of therapy ourselves, we decided to leave the Tucuxi to their amusements and headed for Lagoa da Prata and the reported *botos* there, the animals we had originally come to see. This little episode was best forgotten. One of the many ridiculous scenarios you'll never read about in any respectable publication about professionals in the field is of Flip and me out on that lake in that tiny pedal boat trying to take pictures of a couple of pint-sized fresh water dolphins who, flushed with sexual frenzy, were trying desperately to mate with the silly contraption. That belongs in the repressed memory file.

Revenge of the Devil Dolphins

It turned out Lagoa da Prata was a fair distance to the south, near the city of Belo Horizonte, and required a substantial airplane trip, but that was good, we needed a break to regroup. It would be like starting over. We could refocus and compose ourselves and carry on like the professionals we knew we could be.

Belo Horizonte turned out to be a thriving, sprawling city, the capital of the mining district of Brazil. The perfect place to revitalize and refresh, check out a few of their famous gem markets, and start anew on our quest for underwater *boto* shots.

We settled in and made arrangements for a car to take us the next day to the resort near where the dolphins were rumored to be, exceedingly curious, but

14

frankly a bit skeptical. After all, this wasn't exactly where we had originally thought we would find these animals, and the enterprise had a distinct odor of a wild goose chase about it, but we were committed now, and were determined to see it through.

After a relaxing evening in delightful Belo Horizonte we arrived at the place the following afternoon. It was a resort on the Rio Sao Francisco (San Francisco River). They had dammed the river to make the small lake and imported white sand to make a beautiful beach, which was crowded with swimmers and sun bathers (and was the first place I had seen women wearing thong bikinis, which are now commonplace everywhere, but back then it was a revelation).

Except for the additional scenery, it seemed a typical holiday setting, sun umbrellas and colorful beach blankets spread out in random patterns, kids running and kicking sand on protesting adults, sun reflecting off of the water. But it was all about to change.

The tranquil scene was shattered by an agonized scream, blood-curdling as they say. Everyone froze, not sure what was happening or where it was coming from, not sure what direction to run, but pretty sure they wanted to run somewhere. Then the scream came again. It was coming from a short distance offshore where a middle-aged portly man (also wearing a thong bathing suit, incredibly) was trying his best to scale a slippery piling sticking up from the lake bottom. It looked like he was making good progress, too, hands and one foot scrabbling crab-like for purchase on the slimy wood. He probably would have made it, but one leg seemed to be held fast underwater. Down he went, but then popped up again like a Poseidon missile, hands and arms wind-milling against the slippery surface. It was obvious

15

something was dragging his right leg down, and then we all saw it just for a second as his leg came clear momentarily of the water…a gnarly gray *thing* was on the screaming man's leg. It looked like a rough stick, clamped around his ankle.

He went down again with a splash, the screams gurgling into silence for a moment, then he was back up again, screaming and rolling and thrashing. A long gray shape disengaged itself and glided away underwater, a small dorsal fin breaking the surface as it disappeared.

Before anyone could react, a figure was racing through the crowd, some sort of hotel employee judging by his khaki uniform. He splashed toward the struggling man, dragged him ashore, and immediately escorted him limping and moaning into a small maintenance building just off the beach.

The crowd gradually calmed and, milling and murmuring, went back about their holiday business on the beach, staying clear of the water now.

Flip and I looked at each other wide-eyed. What the hell was *that*?

We made our way to the little building and warily peeked inside.

The victim was lying back on a cot, babbling a steady stream of what had to be Portuguese curse words, while the hotel guy was dabbing antiseptic on numerous bite marks on his leg. They didn't look too bad. The skin was only slightly broken in a few places, but there were a bunch of them; it looked more like a deliberate gnawing than a bite.

Flip introduced himself, brandishing some official-looking *National Geographic* credentials (these generally worked wonders everywhere we went, a universal welcome card). The hotel guy spoke some

16

English, and he started to fill us in on what was going on.

It seemed these dolphins *had* been introduced here to mitigate the piranha problem; people generally didn't like swimming with piranhas, and the folks around here figured that if it became known that the fish were in their swimming waters, it could be bad for business. Besides, the *botos* themselves would probably serve as a tourist attraction, so they were looking at an all-around win. And the idea worked great, as far as it went.

The *botos* did eat the piranhas. All of them. And they did draw attention. The resort took to feeding the newcomers after the piranhas were gone, and the dolphins began to interact with the guests, and the guests with them. After a time, children (the hotel guy said) began to tease and torment the animals, and they eventually turned mean and unpredictable. They had taken to ambushing swimmers and waders, grabbing their legs with their sharp teeth and shaking back and forth much like a dog with a rag. (He lifted up his pant leg and showed us his shins criss-crossed with light cuts and scars). He said they didn't bite hard, just hard enough to hang on and scare the be-Jesus out of the leg's owner, much like this unfortunate bethonged victim here, who was still moaning and blubbering a bit.

He said that as the beach maintenance man, by default he had become the custodian of the *botos*, taking on their feeding and trying to steer them away from guests, but occasionally one or both of them would slip through his vigilance and launch an attack like the one we had just witnessed. It didn't bode well for their continued stay here, he was afraid, which was too bad, because he had grown grudgingly fond of them. (We got

17

the sense he was rooting for the dolphins over the guests, but he didn't say that in so many words).

This presented an opportunity for us, however, for here they were. *Botos* in clear water. These guys weren't the vivid pink color of the ones in the Rio Negro, more a mottled grayish brown, something to do with their shrimp-poor diet, but they were *botos* nonetheless.

Flip arranged with the guy to meet us there in the morning when he fed the animals, and we could try for some underwater shots. We couldn't believe our luck. Incredible. The psychic crystal lady had been telling the truth. The maintenance guy said she had been through here a couple of months ago, before the bad behavior started, but he wasn't sure how the communication experiment had gone.

Botos Gone Bad – or The Couple That Preys Together...

We showed up bright and early in front of the little shed the next morning, cameras and snorkel gear in hand. Our guy was just wading back to shore, a couple of big plastic buckets in hand from which he had just dumped fish and scraps a little ways out, and we could see the two dolphins thrashing and splashing around as they fed. In the clear water you could see now that they were different-looking, though, not like the familiar streamlined dolphin shape we were used to. They had these long, gnarly snouts, full of twisted teeth, which was what we had seen clamped around the guy's leg yesterday. It was almost like these were an earlier version of the modern animals, a proto-dolphin somehow survived here in fresh water, like discovering a Neanderthal living in the basement of your building. The similarities were there, but you had to appreciate the refinements of the later versions.

18

It was a beautiful morning, though, and the water was crystal clear, nobody else was around...conditions couldn't have been better.

Our guy had a few words of warning, however. These things were ill-tempered and cunning, he was telling us. Try to keep them both in sight, was his advice. Keeping that in mind, we started wading out and immediately lost sight of both of them. They just glided away. We got out a little over waist deep and reconnoitered, Flip looking under water while I scanned the surface, both of us feeling a little silly standing around out there with our gear; luckily, none of the hotel guests were out to see us yet.

Soon, Flip saw something underwater ahead of us. One of the *botos* was cruising back and forth. As the good assistant, I was standing behind, carrying the gear, the different housings, and cameras. He turned, and I handed him the camera he asked for, but when he looked again, the dolphin had disappeared. Odd, it was just there. Now we were both looking underwater, and, sure enough, the *boto* reappeared right in front of us. A split-second later the world exploded.

Something large clamped painfully down on my leg. Before my mind could process that it surely was the second *boto* that had sneaked around behind us and grabbed me, I was shrieking and thrashing around in the water in a complete panic, just like the guy on the pole the day before, the survival portion of the brain stem completely in charge. Of course this completely ruined the shot, scared the hell out of Flip, and complete chaos ensued.

The thing finally let go, but not right away, and not before we had a chance to visit, this animal and I. And it wasn't pretty. For one thing, its twisted, gnarly beak was filled with ragged yellow teeth, and it actually had little hairs sticking out of it—scary. The wacky new age psychic lady may have been having some luck communicating with these dolphins using crystals, but at the moment, I was wishing I had a crystal, or any other long, sharp object I could use to jab the sucker in the snout so it would let go of my leg.

I was looking into the beady little eye of a fellow mammal, but there was something disturbing about it. There was something askew here, a mean Snopes-like cold cleverness and indifference, a lack of humanity, if that makes sense, or any fellow mammal warmth. If this were a neighborhood kid you were looking at instead of a dolphin, you'd just know he'd end up in prison for knocking over a string of convenience stores, or worse.

As I was yelling and thrashing about, Flip was lurching around off balance trying to figure out what was going on; meanwhile, the maintenance guy was splashing through the shallows rushing out to help. It was quite a show, we could have charged admission. I now empathized completely with the guy climbing the pole...having a large animal grab you unexpectedly sets off some primal mechanism that is out of your control.

The thing finally released me and finned away. We made our way ashore to recover, and I now had matching marks on my left leg that were starting to look familiar.

We soon found out that this was the dolphins' modus operandi; one would act as bait, distracting and luring the victims along, while the other evil-doer circled around behind for the attack. Brilliant.

We found this out only because when we went back out later that morning the same thing happened,

20

only this time it was Flip who got nailed. This was unnerving. I, for one, was getting a little jumpy out there.

We finally settled on a counter-strategy; the only way we were going to get any close-ups was by having one of us go as counter-bait. (Me. Reluctantly. But, as Flip pointed out, he was the principal here, I was the assistant; he encouraged me to read the fine print of my contract. Besides, he couldn't concentrate on taking any pictures with that thing hanging on his leg, it really hurt).

The plan was simple. We would get set up, pretend we were engaged with watching the first *boto*, me behind as a target, and then quickly turn and photograph the second one as it swooped in for the attack. It worked perfectly, but there was no way to prevent the attack from being consummated. I tried to switch legs to even out the damage, but that didn't always work, the botos must have been loving it, easy stupid prey.

Flip was getting lots of shots; plenty I thought...more than enough in my opinion...and the *botos* were clearly starting to enjoy this. We repeated the process several times. But every time I thought surely that last session was the end, he would mumble something about trying another F-stop or something and the nightmare would begin again. The next thing I knew the damned thing would dart in and start worrying my leg again like a terrier with a bone, looking up with glee from that little piggy eye.

And then I snapped. I'm not proud of this...a truly first class assistant would have stayed until the light failed or the film ran out...but I bolted. I guess I went on strike. (That's how Flip would describe it in telling the story later.) But I'd had it. After a particularly vicious mauling, I couldn't take anymore, and I took off, splashing my way to shore, howling, "That does it!", or something to that effect.

Everyone was very understanding. The hotel guy tended to my wounds, (just scratches really, I thought they would be much worse), and Flip agreed that we had gotten what we came for, (at least that's what he told me, eying me I thought somewhat warily), that there was no need to go back out there.

I was glad. I wasn't sure I could have gone back into the Lagoa da Prata with those nasty brutes at large. And I was creeped out, in large part because of that look in their eyes as they were chewing on me.

We packed up and readied ourselves for the trip home.

Reflections in a Beady Eye

The flight home was quiet. I didn't need any more excitement at the moment. The slight facial tic I had recently developed was abating somewhat, my bandaged shins had stopped oozing, the onboard cocktail service was prompt, all was returning to normal, and I had time to reflect.

I kept coming back to the old maxim: "Be careful what you wish for..." I had wanted to get close to those fresh water dolphins and see what they were all about. The behavior of those particular *botos*, as well as the behavior of the little Tucuxi's, was frankly disturbing. But, to be fair, they were like captive animals in a zoo, not representative of the creatures in the wild...all the more argument against keeping wild animals confined.

But, still, I couldn't get those eyes out of my memory. I'm sure it is doing a disservice to all of the well-adjusted and well-meaning dolphins of the world, but to my mind, that particular creature was not the helpful dolphin you often hear about who would nudge you gently ashore if it found you drowning in the surf, that much was clear. Far from it. I needed to reacquaint myself with a better sort of cetacean. I had seen all of the *botos* I cared to see for the moment, thank you.

The Road To Trincomalee

I really did know better. Or certainly should have. These days most of us are more careful about plunging blissfully off into the unknown without doing any preliminary research. But back in the day it didn't seem to be an issue. I think it had something to do with us being a lot younger and having a higher tolerance for adventure. In those days when I would get a wild offer from Flip Nicklin to be an assistant on one of his *National Geographic* projects in some far-flung place, there was no hesitating. It was a chance to go somewhere I had never been, and I figured the details could sort themselves out later.

I was working as a captain for Exploration Cruise Lines at the time, and they were good about giving me leaves of absence when Flip would call needing a captain/diving assistant/sherpa for one of his photo shoots, and I would jump at the chance whenever possible.

Flip was on assignment off the east coast of Sri Lanka, thrashing around on a tiny sailboat with whale researcher Hal Whitehead, following sperm whales and the odd blue whale (and probably getting some real work done). But the enterprise was about to morph into one of those whale-related side trips involving a large chartered sailboat and a movie film crew, so there was a need for me as an assistant.

Flip left me a message in another static-filled phone call; he was going to be out on the sailboat with Hal longer than he had thought, but he could meet me at a resort he had been using as a home base in Trincomalee, Sri Lanka, a few days after I got there, and we would hook up with the film people from there.

I had made my hurried air travel plans and secured a night's lodging near the Colombo airport through a travel agent friend, not really planning much beyond that for the moment. Trincomalee was on the other side of the island from Colombo, but I planned to simply make my arrangements to travel across to rendezvous with Flip after I arrived.

The flight to Colombo turned out to involve a four-hour layover stop in Singapore (which allowed me a sightseeing visit to the famous Raffles bar to sample the original Singapore Sling), but I managed to avoid any caning offenses ashore and caught the later flight on to Sri Lanka.

I mention the beverage-sampling stop only to explain why it follows that I wasn't in the most sterling of moods when we touched down in Colombo hours later that night in the middle of a downpour of monstrous proportions. I had never experienced monsoon rains before, and the lack of any covered jet way between the plane and the airport assured all of us Godforsaken passengers a full appreciation of a real equatorial drenching by the time we dog-paddled our way to shelter. The baggage area was really just a big covered shed, with various stalls set up around the perimeter, and masses of people going busily about God-knows-what at that hour, and in that stifling heat and humidity. The atmosphere was thick, not just as in a figure of speech, it was like breathing underwater. Head pounding, I was, as I said, beginning to regret my Raffles interlude.

I breast stroked my way toward the most prominent stall, a currency exchange, for my first encounter with one of the few malevolent Sri Lankans I was to meet. I later found the Sri Lankan people to be almost always smiling, pleasant, helpful, and usually ready with that charming universal aloha greeting "Mahatmaya," accompanied by the characteristic head wobble that to our eyes is neither a nod yes, nor a head shake no, but something in between whose meaning still baffles me. But this scowling little man was none of these things, and his head wasn't wobbling charmingly, or indeed in any other way. In fact he was studying me with an alarming expression.

I tried exchanging pleasantries with him as I filled out a couple of traveler's checks to trade for local currency and slid them over, but I wasn't making much headway. I didn't speak any Sinhalese, and he didn't appear to respond to my efforts in any other language, including my deferential don't-cheat-me-I'm-just-a-hapless-foreigner body language, so I just stood by quietly sweating while he took my checks and pushed a massive pile of wrinkled rupee notes my way and then sat steadily observing me across the counter. I had checked the exchange rate, (surprisingly), before leaving home, so with a sigh resigned myself to sorting and counting the mess in front of me. As soon as I began counting and laying out rows of different denominations, the evil little man gave a quick start and hurriedly pushed another equally large pile of rumpled notes my way. I was appalled. At this point our non-verbal communication took a decided turn for the worse, as menacing eye contact replaced our former civilized pantomime. I began making large bundles of rupee notes and stuffing them into various pockets as I worked my way through the heap of bills.

Satisfied that I had finally gotten reasonably close to a fair exchange, and padded with wads of rupee notes, I left my new friend and waddled over to the baggage area to claim my duffel bag. Armed with my bag, I slogged my way back out into the downpour to hail a cab to take me to town and my hotel. I had a voucher for my hotel that the cab driver acknowledged with a head wobble and a smile, and off we went.

It was really when I exited the cab in downtown Colombo that it struck me that Sri Lanka had a quality of "foreignness" that was unfamiliar to me. I had at that time traveled a bit in Central and South America, and some in Europe, but looking out at that rainy night in Colombo gave me the first of several "not in Kansas anymore" moments I was to experience in the coming days.

The city was incredibly busy and crowded, even in the middle of the night. Insanely busy, kicked-an-anthill busy, and colorful, noisy and odiferous, but somehow askew, a parallel universe that appeared at first glance to be like the one I had just left, but with an underlying strangeness I couldn't quite place. Crowds of uniformly Indian looking faces surged through the streets, some with the Hindu bindi spot on the forehead, speaking languages whose sounds were totally unfamiliar to me. No other Westerner was in sight. There were signs and billboards whose non-Roman letters gave me

27

no clue to their meaning, presumably advertising goods and movies and services that sparked not a shred of recognition. There were a few signs in English too, however, and luckily one of them was for my hotel, the Orient Sapphire, a seedy-looking downtown hotel drooping and dripping at the edges. The concept of a dry room with a bed held enormous appeal for me at the moment. I peeled a couple of rupee notes off of one of my bundles, paid the cabbie, mahatmaya, and jostled my way in through the entrance doors and into the dark lobby. I sloshed my way to the lighted reception desk, presented my reservation voucher to the sleepy looking clerk, and again produced one of those ungainly wads of money from a pocket and began counting out bills.

It was at this point that I became aware of other people in the darkness of the lobby, lots of them, lurking quietly, watching me idiotically standing in a pool of light holding a big wad of cash. I could visualize myself frozen with a bovine expression on my face with a prominent "FAIR GAME" sign on my back in the appropriate language. I fancied the atmosphere here turning sinister.

In silence I sheepishly finished the transaction with the clerk, returned the big wad of money to my pocket, and slunk off to my room up the stairs, seeing in my paranoid mind's eye countless pairs of eyes following my every move and plotting the inevitable mugging to come.

I survived the trip to my room, bolted myself in, started breathing again, and had a look around. It was a shabby, depressing affair, a small bed covered by a mosquito net canopy, a dresser, a small bath, worn linoleum, and all starkly lit by a single light fixture high on the ceiling. But I was so beat at that point that I threw my bag in a corner, crawled fully clothed under the mosquito net, and, ignoring the imagined shadowy figures creeping around outside the net, resigned myself to sleep. Tomorrow I would figure out how to get from here across the country to Trincomalee.

Civil war? What civil war?

The next morning was a marked improvement, a new day, a new planet. The sun was shining and all of the people I encountered in the hotel were chock full of remarkably good will. I had no idea where that imagined scabrous group of villains from the night before had crawled off to, but there was no hint of them this morning.

After a delightful breakfast in the hotel dining room with the pleasant staff, mahatmaya, and feeling pretty damned good, considering, I settled up my bill and caught a cab back out to the airport to book the advertised shuttle flight to Trincomalee, the confident world traveler going about his business.

The airport shuttle area was deserted. When I finally found a lone attendant he informed me that all shuttle flights were canceled "because of the troubles". I wasn't able to discern exactly what "the troubles" were, my communication level just wasn't up to it, but apparently there had been some recent unpleasantness that made going to Trincomalee inadvisable. I had read somewhere that there was long standing animosity in Sri Lanka between the majority Sinhalese, who are Buddhist, and the Hindu Tamil minority (although the religious difference was seemingly just one aspect of the complex problem). It was one of those long-standing ethnic and religious conflicts that seemed so needless and inexplicable to an outsider, but the dangerous details had escaped me. It turned out a group called the Tamil Tigers had recently attacked and blown up a number of areas

29

near where I wanted to go, but I naively hadn't made it my business to know that at the time. I communicated to the attendant to the best of my ability my urgent desire to get to Trincomalee, lots of beseeching looks and hand gestures on my part, followed by sympathetic shrugs and "so-sorrys" in response. Finally it was established that if I really wanted to travel across the island, there was a bus that was still going, and directions to the bus terminal were conveyed, head wobbles were exchanged, and I was off in another taxi.

The bus terminal turned out to be a big, hot, muddy, and diesel-stained lot full of brightly painted old buses on the outskirts of town, with another open air shed serving as the terminal. Ticket purchased, I was then directed to an empty old bus at the edge of the lot where it was indicated I could wait the three hours or so until departure time. So climbing aboard, and opening all of the windows to let out some of the heat, I threw my bag down on one of the bench seats and settled in for a sweaty nap.

On the Road

I awoke to a persistent, albeit gentle, prodding on my leg, and was surprised upon opening my eyes to see my empty bus now nearly full, with rows of patient, brightly clothed people quietly watching an ancient man methodically poking me as I lay sprawled out on the bench seat. I put my bag on my lap and made room for my fellow travelers, the old man, and his equally ossified companion, who both fell asleep after sitting down, leaving me still the object of attention, but with the vague feeling that I was something of a letdown now that I was no longer being prodded.

I could still see I was being politely scrutinized, however, being the only pale face in sight, as more

30

people streamed aboard, solemn families carrying all manner of things, brightly gowned demure ladies and children traveling with dignified men. Finally, when it seemed every seat was taken, the driver appeared, and without a backward glance at us, or our tickets, pulled the door closed and we started off.

I was transfixed at the window as we made our way out of Colombo and toward the interior. At first the roads were jammed with people and carts and dogs and cabs and buses, swarming and surging like tides up and down the side streets, until we made our way to the outskirts of the city, traffic thinned, and we were making our way through an increasingly beautiful countryside. Magical things began to appear: a tree full of huge hanging bats lifted as one into the air as we passed, a boy earnestly washed an elephant in a roadside stream. Women sat on colorful rugs alongside the roadway selling clothing and jewelry and piles of spices. The air became cooler as we ground our way uphill and gained altitude, and the green hills waved gently away into the distance. The houses became less numerous and gave way to estates. Passing one well-tended house, I looked down into a walled yard at a gathering of somber people lined up mournfully around a large rectangular fire which I had to assume was a funeral pyre. At one crossroads we had to stop and wait for a large elephant to drag a log across the road. Tea plantations began to appear—neat, orderly, cultivated fields.

I sat with my face pressed against the window for probably several hours. I must have been quite a sight from the road, this pale western face staring goggle-eyed from the painted bus as we rollicked along. We passed temples and huge stone Buddhas, and towns with names like Kandy and Dambulla, while orange-robed monks wandered in and out of sight along the side roads. I was shaken from my trance only when we finally pulled over at an open-air roadhouse restaurant for a refreshment break. It was a charming place, with tablecloths and settings on the little tables and smiling waiters. The food smelled wonderful. This was my first traditional Sri Lankan curry meal, and it was unforgettable.

There were numerous bowls of different curry concoctions, I think seven is the traditional number, and stacks of soft, round pancake-type breads called "hoppers" into which the curry mix is spooned and eaten, and tea and beer. I was in heaven. I had no idea what different kinds of curry the bowls contained. I did pull a couple of fish bones out of one, but all were delicious. There is nothing like the feeling of good cheer you get from being in a foreign place, eating the local fare, and feeling an empathy with your fellow humans that transcends language and customs. And sharing several large bottles of local beer with your new friends seems to help immensely with this. I almost hated to leave when the bus driver finally began to gather his flock and shepherd us back aboard. But the idyllic tone of the trip was about to change.

Going Downhill

After traveling some miles through flat, wooded country, we started downhill just as it was starting to get dark. In one of the little towns we passed there suddenly appeared a recently burned out concrete government building that occasioned a lot of talk and pointing among the other passengers. The windows were blown out and black streaks of soot snaked upward from the empty window sockets. The mood on the bus became somber, and it became clear to me that this had something to do with the "troubles" that the attendant had mentioned at the airport. We continued into the twilight a much quieter bus. It was just about completely dark when the bus came to a shuddering stop alongside the road. The bus became quieter still when the driver pulled a greasy toolbox out from under his seat and set out into the night with a grim look.

The minutes dragged on, ten and then twenty, and I finally ventured outside, along with other male passengers, to uneasily stand vigil around several pairs of legs sticking out from beneath the engine compartment as tools and flashlights were passed back and forth, and much commentary was exchanged in Sinhalese. I wasn't happy about the way many of the men were keeping a wary eye on the darkness around us, and I was totally at a loss as to what was going on under the bus. From the plumbing and parts that appeared at intervals, to be examined and discussed over, I was pretty sure it was the air compressor that was the focus of the concern. Since the only two things on a bus that need an air compressor to operate are the air horn and the air brakes, I shared in the concern. I wasn't going to miss the horn all that much, in fact it seemed like the last thing we needed at the moment, but since the road was tending definitely downhill, I was missing the brakes already.

It seemed odd to me that there was no other traffic on the road. Then, it started to rain again. The warm feeling of well being I was enjoying only an hour ago was undergoing some serious erosion at this point. And I wasn't alone; I could also see concern on the faces around me. But, finally, with much discussion, all of the parts got reassembled and replaced, the bus was started,

33

a few test starts and stops were conducted, and with all apparently back in good order we started off again.

As we made our way through the rainy darkness, I remember finding it odd that I didn't see any electric lights outside, just an occasional light that looked like open flame in the distance through the rainy windows. Buildings began to appear out of the gloom; we were obviously entering a town, but the power seemed to be out. Candles and lanterns lighted doorways and windows, and it was raining heavily now. We seemed to leave the town behind, and suddenly the bus pulled into what looked like a muddy, empty field and stopped.

The other passengers were animated now, gathering up their belongings and exiting the bus, people were materializing to meet them, and the occasional odd boxy-looking car pulled up and gathered someone in. I wasn't sure what I was expecting, but it wasn't this muddy field in the middle of nowhere in the middle of the night, with not a building or taxi stand in sight.

The rest of the passengers dissolved into the night, the bus sloshed away, and it was then that it struck me, the situation I had finally put myself in. My naïve blundering along with no real plan, enjoying the fact that I had no plan, had finally led me here, at a loss, standing in the middle of a dark, muddy field in the rain, in the most foreign place I could ever imagine with no communication skills and no clear path to move forward. I had no one to blame but myself.

Salivation

I started slogging my way in what I hoped was the direction of town, hoping to find some place to get out of the rain, maybe to hide out until morning when I could try to regain my bearings and find this rendezvous place Flip had told me about.

It was dark, and I was soaked now, bag and self, thoroughly miserable. Then, I noticed another of those unfamiliar boxy-looking cars idling alongside the now otherwise-empty field. With a sense of unreality and a feeling there was nothing left to lose, I approached the car, tapped on the window, and proffered up my soggy notes from Flip with the name of the rendezvous place, the Ocean Club, to the car's occupant, although I thought the prospect of actually finding anything resembling a club or resort in this present situation was absurd. I was incredibly heartened by a friendly face peering through the car window, who seemed to recognize the English place name, and who waved me around to the passenger side door. Weighing the prospect of curling up somewhere in the mud to wait for morning against the wisdom of jumping into a strange car in a foreign place, I threw my bag in and hopped in behind it.

What brought the car and its occupant to the field I will never know…maybe he was waiting for someone who didn't arrive on the bus. But whatever the reason, we had both now committed ourselves, and we started off into the rainy darkness. My sense of unreality grew as we turned toward what I thought was the opposite direction from town. The rain-covered passenger side windshield was lacking a windshield wiper and was impossible to see anything through, and the inside was fogging up, so I soon had no sense of direction as we sped through the increasing downpour.

We established that we shared no common communication ground whatsoever beyond the name "Ocean Club," this pleasant looking middle-aged Sri Lankan man and I, which we repeated back and forth several times as we sped along. This seemed more and

35

more surreal to me, not helped by the fact that I couldn't make out anything outside the windows. I had the sense of being in a foreign space capsule heading to some unknown destination. Not that I was feeling uncomfortable or in particular danger, just completely adrift from my moorings. (Like those tales of alien abductions, would I ever see home again?) I vowed I would never allow myself to be put into such an out-of-control situation again.

We traveled miles through what seemed to be utter wet blackness, when finally I was just able to make out a distant light through the windshield. The light grew nearer, electric lights I could make out now through the foggy glass; it was a guard shack with a red and white barrier pole stretched across the road.

We pulled up to the shack, my friend rolled down his window, exchanged some words with the guard, the pole went up, and we were waved through, and I was back in my underwater world of foggy windows. There were more blurry lights now, and structures, and suddenly we pulled under some brightly lit shelter and stopped.

I opened the car door and what I saw amazed me almost as much as if I *had* been abducted and arrived on another planet. We were stopped under a modern looking hotel portico, and a smartly dressed doorman was hurrying our way. White concrete steps led up to glass doors behind which I could see a carpeted lobby with potted plants and a check-in desk.

The doorman grabbed my bag, held the car door for me, and uttered probably the most unexpected words I had ever heard: "Captain Bennett? We've been expecting you!"

In dream-like slow motion, my new savior friend refused my grateful offer of money, and, to my regret, I did not get his name. With some amiable words to the doorman and me, he drove off into the night, and I don't know how to thank this good-hearted Samaritan. I was escorted inside, checked in, and led to the restaurant where dinner and a bottle of wine awaited me. (I was apparently the only guest in the resort, a symptom of "the troubles.") Flip was to return in a couple of days, but for now my bungalow awaited me, and I was to let the staff know whatever I needed. I was gently scolded about using the dangerous public transportation; private car and driver were the recommended mode of getting about, and only in daylight.

After the late dinner, suffused with a sense of profound, if undeserved, salvation, well fed and wined, I made my way to my bungalow a grateful pilgrim. We had many more adventures ahead of us here, from poison peanuts to suspicions of gunrunning at sea, but nothing compared to the feeling I had upon finally reaching our temporary home here in Trincomalee. Safe for the moment, and with thanks to whatever benign Buddha or multi-armed deity might be assigned to looking after travelers and fools in Sri Lanka, I fell into bed and slept like a babe.

The Sailing Whales of Patagonia

The Lure of the South

The timing was going to work out perfectly. I had just
finished up the Alaska season on the ship I was working
on, so I had a block of vacation time ahead of me. I got
the message from Flip that he was heading to Argentina
on a *National Geographic* assignment to cover Dr. Roger
Payne's study of the Southern Right Whales at Peninsula
Valdes, and he needed a diving assistant.

I was looking forward to seeing Dr. Payne again.
The last time I had seen Roger was in Hawaii when he
had lashed himself to the top of the wheelhouse of a
boat I was running on a memorable trip back into
Lahaina during a sudden storm.

This had taken place a few years earlier. We had
been out off the coast of West Maui recording
Humpback Whale songs on Tad Luckey's old boat Sport
Diver when the weather started picking up.

It was a good idea to head for home when the
wind picked up out there because the entrance into
Lahaina Harbor had a nasty tendency to close out during
westerly swells, meaning that waves would begin
breaking all the way down the channel into the harbor,
ending in an almost 90 degree slew to the right around

the breakwater into the boat basin. It was beginning to blow, so we figured we were in for a ride. Adding to the excitement was the way the harbor had to be approached with that particular boat. Sport Diver had a single engine, a wide flat bottom, and an undersized rudder, which meant that in those heavy sea conditions you had to keep full power on all the way into and through the turn or you could end up being swept onto the concrete pier at the end of the channel.

It wasn't really as bad as it sounds, as long as you didn't lose your nerve and cut power at the last minute, or there wasn't another boat coming out around the corner, or something on the boat didn't break or quit. But even so, it wasn't for the faint of heart, and most people, understandably, white-knuckled it all the way in, and then let their heart rate slow over some cordials at the bar at Kimo's Restaurant.

It frightened most, but not Roger. We began hearing these wild yowls coming from the top of the boat just as we timed our dash in and started down the channel. Looking out the windows and up we could see him standing shirtless in the storm on top of the upper deck with a dock line tied around his middle, head back and howling. A little disconcerting, but he had the best view of the whole operation up there, and he seemed non-plussed after we surfed around the corner and tied back up at the slip. Just another routine boat ride. Dr. Payne was not the typical button-down academic type.

I was looking forward to this Patagonian adventure. Since I was already planning to be in Boston over the next few days visiting friends, Flip and I arranged to meet at the Geographic headquarters in Washington the next week to gather up our documents and gear and head south.

39

We ended up with first class tickets all the way to Buenos Aires where we were to pick up a rental car for the drive south to Patagonia. We had their blessings and the tickets and we were off.

We collected tents and gear and underwater camera housings and film, and I went shopping for my roughing-it-in-the-wild clothes and boots and bags. We gathered all of our stuff together, along with a fair amount of company cash and documents, stuffed it into various cases and containers, and headed to the airport.

This first-class travel was new to me. Armed with premium tickets and with all of Flip's travel miles, we were pretty much given the airline's equivalent of royal treatment. Special waiting areas and clubs and deference were suddenly open to us, and I was ruined for the rest of my traveling life at a young age. I was particularly taken by the little slippers they gave us for our feet.

In the Lapdance of Luxury

We arrived in Buenos Aires remarkably refreshed and ready for a night on the town. We had our baggage sent to the hotel, but, maybe as a kind of payback for all of that special service, I discovered I was missing a bag...all of that new in-the-field gear I had just bought in DC. No matter, I still had my tent and sleeping bag and essential items, but, if the bag didn't show up before we headed south, I was going to be a bit underdressed for the wilds of Patagonia. So I hung onto the airline slippers, they might come in handy for shuffling around camp.

Sailing out from our downtown hotel into the city that night, I was struck by how cosmopolitan and European Buenos Aires was. A beautiful city on the banks of the wide Rio de Plata River, full of upscale shops and restaurants and beautiful people. But I swear there was this slight pervasive odor of boiling meat, or tallow, everywhere we went, so faint I thought it could be my imagination, but it seemed to be everywhere. It was definitely a beef-centric country, though, and we headed straight for a carne restaurant to check it out. The restaurant we chose was definitely not for the veggie-squeamish. Two full-sized stuffed Hereford steers flanked the entryway, and the first things that greeted the entering diner were stacks of different cuts of meat and organs piled high behind steamy glass for the gastronome's viewing pleasure. I'm no vegetarian, but this was enough to give even me a slight appetite check.

We were taken into the dark interior and shown to our table by a tall, gaunt waiter, serious and pale-faced with slicked back hair and a noticeable limp. The large dining area was dark, smoky wood, Bavarian looking, with old cuckoo clocks on the walls. All of the waiters looked similar to ours, and they were shuffling around in the half-light with serious expressions. I felt like I was playing a double agent in an old World War II movie.

We ordered an appetizer of raw steak carpaccio, some red Argentine wine, and looked over the selection of meat offerings.

It appeared you could eat just about any cow body part imaginable, prepared any number of ways. Our waiter recommended a cut of meat called "cola," which sounded reassuringly familiar, so we both went for it, medio-rojo, por favor. It turns out "cola" means "tail" in Spanish.

The things that arrived some minutes later didn't resemble steaks, more like roasts or rumps or big globes of meat. They were huge. Almost round, they sizzled and quivered there in the center of the giant plates. A guy hurried over, a head waiter or meat inspector or

41

something, checked everything out; apparently all was in order, and we were free to eat.

We both knifed in with enthusiasm, carving out big chunks and chewing with gusto. It was delicious, perfect. The carnage continued. I imagined getting some approving looks from the otherwise somber waiters passing by. I thought I was making some progress; I could see the halfway point from here. Big gulps of the red wine kept things lubed up and moving along. Soon, I began to flag; I was starting to tire. Flip was still slicing along at good speed, however; he was starting to pull ahead. I carved out a particularly toothsome slice, probably what would be called a cutlet at a more civilized table, and forked it in. That got a friendly nod from the meat inspector who was looking over the plates at a nearby table. I nodded back, encouraged, masticating away. I was definitely beginning to slow down now, however, and I sensed some capacity resistance. It was clear I wasn't going to make it all the way through.

I should have stopped then and there and called for the doggy bag, but 1) I didn't know if they had such a thing here or 2) how to ask for it if they did. Pride and inertia kept me going, knifing and forking, chewing and swallowing bite after endless bite. I glanced up and saw that Flip now had his head down, but was still tucking it doggedly away. But I sensed he too was losing speed. The end was in sight; my meat mound was diminishing; the bare spots on the plate were growing.

Hearing a small groan, I looked up and saw that Flip had indeed polished off his steak ahead of me, but he looked pale and slightly cross-eyed. I downed my last bite and washed it home with a last gulp of wine, then leaned back and wondered what in God's name I had just done. Like a hyena that has just gorged itself beyond reason at the kill, I was gazing in a stupor off into the middle distance.

I don't know how much time passed before I was brought back to the present by the appearance of our grim waiter. No, thank you, I wouldn't be having any dessert. Coffee maybe.

We slunk out of the restaurant back into the night, chastened but wiser. So *that* was a steak dinner in Argentina.

It was now after midnight, so nightlife was just heating up in Buenos Aires. We were told that things don't really get going until 2 or 3 am. There was a brightly lit *Cabaret* sign on what appeared to be a fancy nightclub across the street. We had planned to pick up the car and get an early start the next morning, but thought we'd duck in for a nightcap before heading back to the hotel.

The first sight that greeted us upon entering the place was a feather-covered woman belting out a song from a stage in the center of the room, and the second sight was a row of the most beautiful women imaginable lined up at the bar, dressed in slinky outfits, and seemingly outrageously pleased to see us.

Stunned nearly stupid by the sight, and still reeling from the recent meat-fest, we shuffled our way to the nearest booth and slid in. Three of the loveliest of the collection at the bar glided over to our table and took our drink order, and then one went off presumably to fetch our drinks. The remaining two, to our amazement, slid in next to us.

My new friend was incredible. I don't know if it was the wine or some sort of temporary brain-gout induced by the recent beef overdose, but I was smitten. Time seemed to slow down. Imagine, if you can, a supermodel who is also intelligent, funny, and kind, and smells like springtime in heaven. Her name was Alejandra. We seemed to have stumbled into a high-class bordello, for lack of a better word. But that seemed such an unwholesome description. It didn't seem like a slink-guiltily-upstairs kind of place, but more what I imagined a geisha house might be like. These girls were charming company. Alejandra's halting English was on a par with my halting Spanish. Over drinks, I was beginning to have serious visions of settling down, learning the Tango, and raising up little gauchitos on the estancia. Who knows where this could have led and how much money this could have cost had Flip not, in a moment of fortuitous clarity and with a superhuman effort, drug me forcibly from the place.

Once back out on the street, the enchantment broken, the whole episode seemed like a dream, Odysseus' ship somehow slipped safely past the Sirens. We had to get on the road. The dangers posed by civilization here in Buenos Aires were obviously overwhelming. But it wasn't going to be that easy to escape the city.

The Gaucho Marx Brothers Head South

The next morning dawned clear and calm and beautiful. Opening the hotel window, the pervasive tallow odor of the previous night was no longer distinguishable; we had been assimilated...it was us. I imagined I was off-gassing beef vapor through my pores. Outside it was Springtime for Argentina in November, and the trees lining the wide boulevards were budding out in flowers. Business in the southern hemisphere was getting underway; cars and pedestrians were already jamming the street...surely they were not the same ones

44

who were milling about late last night. When did these people sleep?

Good news; the airline called and they had located my missing bag; it was in Milan, Italy. Now it was official, my luggage was more well traveled than me. It was unclear how long it would take to get the bag to Argentina, but when it arrived they would arrange to transport it south by bus to Puerto Madryn near where Dr. Payne had set up his research camp, so all was theoretically well.

The car rental people called, our car would be delivered to the hotel in an hour. The Geographic Travel Department was a miracle of efficiency. Nothing left for us to do but go downstairs to the hotel restaurant for a meat-laden breakfast and wait for our rental car to arrive.

The car pulled up right on schedule, a new model European job that just held all of our bags and gear and us, it was fortunate we were missing my one bag. We managed to build all of our cases, boxes and assorted gear into stacks filling the trunk and back seat, and we were poised to go. We decided we would trade off driving chores and flipped to see who went first. It was a momentous moment.

I lost the coin toss. I didn't realize what trouble I was in, what driving actually entailed in Argentina. I don't think anyone who hasn't experienced it really could. There were driving rules, but they weren't written down anywhere. The only way to learn the rules was by trial and terror, in the field of combat.

Infused with a misplaced sense of calm confidence, we got into the car, adjusted seats and mirrors and such, unfolded a map, fiddled with the radio, and eased our way into traffic hell.

45

First rule; marked lanes were meaningless. Sure, there were lines painted on the street, but as far as I could tell they signified nothing. Basically as many vehicles as the various drivers present on-scene determined would fit on the roadway at any given time were free to make their way along as rapidly as possible. It was terrifying. There may have been horns blaring, but if there were they were drowned out by the screaming coming from inside our car. Rocketing along at the speed of the traffic, (going any slower would be suicide), I began hyperventilating and sweating bouillon-scented bullets. The second rule, (the most important one, which we didn't figure out until some time later), was that, regardless of any other circumstance, if a rival car pulled even slightly ahead of yours, (determined I believe by relative side mirror location), then that car had free license to perform any maneuver he or she saw fit, up to and including suddenly swerving to cut you off, without the requirement of any warning or eye contact. (In fact any kind of eye contact at all seemed to be generally avoided, probably interpreted as a sign of weakness or a willingness to negotiate.) Of course your car had that option as well if you pulled slightly ahead of the other guy, but it took awhile to get into that carefree, go-to-hell competitive mode and get the hang of it.

Darting for openings in traffic, mashing on the brakes periodically to avoid plowing into a car that just cut you off, leaning on the horn when you had a free moment, it was invigorating motoring and not for the timid, or for anyone with tremors, high blood pressure, or even slightly elevated cholesterol for that matter.

We seemed to be describing ever-widening circles as we tried to make our way out of Buenos Aires, escaped from Sirens only to be caught in a whirlpool.

Trying to look in all directions at once for oncoming carmakazies, hoping somehow to find the highway going south, we kept passing a turnoff for someplace named, (I swear this is true), Moron. We had no intention of going there; we were desperately trying to avoid it. It was then, in the midst of the madness, that I noticed a curious phenomenon. About every third car seemed to be a late-sixties model Ford Falcon. It seemed strange. I didn't have much time to reflect upon this at the time, however, but I found out later that Argentina had purchased and imported the contents of an entire outdated Ford Falcon factory: assembly lines, tooling, parts and all, and they were churning out Argentine Falcons at a furious rate, the people's car, and a true classic at that.

We finally reached escape velocity in our frantic circling; we found the right exit and were slung off onto the highway south towards Mar de Plata and the Pampas.

Those Pampas Fools

The countryside south of the city was placid and beautiful, cattle country, flat grasslands rolling away to the horizon. That wasn't all that was rolling away to the horizon, though. Traffic was still barreling along the two lane highway, smoky Mercedes Benz trucks and Falcons for the most part, everybody ratcheting along at top speed and passing anything even marginally slower than themselves, and squeezing back into their lane at the last possible moment with mere inches to spare. But after the insanity of the city driving, it seemed almost sedate; at least we could look around a bit.

It felt big. Big sky, big fields, big ranches. You could see cattle grazing in every direction, occasional groups of outbuildings far off away from the road, expansive views of gentle grassy hills. But where were

47

the people? I had a keen desire to see a gaucho, the Martin Fierro character with the flat brimmed hat and the insouciant attitude. Probably just like any typical tourist in the American West expecting to see a cowboy. Too many books and movies, no doubt. But it all seemed incomplete, somehow, invalid, until I could lay eyes on a real-life gaucho.

The scene changed briefly as we passed through the resort city of Mar de Plata, with its beautiful beaches, seaside hotels, and throngs of happy families milling about on holiday.

But we had no time for such idle frivolity; we had urgent business with whales to the south. Pressing on, we were soon back into the Pampas country as we made our way down the coast. The country became drier as we passed through the port city of Bahia Blanca and motored past innumerable small towns with dusty dirt side streets. There were still cattle grazing everywhere you looked, but, instead of the earlier grassy fields, the land began to take on an American Southwest high desert look, filled with low scrub similar to sage or chaparral. Horsebacked riders could be seen in the distance working dusty groups of cattle, but never close enough to make them out. Gaucho sighting was proving difficult; they were approaching myth-like status in my mind.

Flip had driving instructions to the research camp and a hand-drawn map from Roger we consulted as we approached the town of Puerto Madryn and the turn-off to the Valdes peninsula.

Puerto Madryn was a compact dusty port town we would come to know well in the coming weeks. There was the typical town square that held most of the population promenading in the evenings, surrounded by

48

cafes, several shops selling leather goods, the telephone exchange, ice cream stands, a drugstore, and, an unexpected surprise, a pizza parlor. Farther away from the square was the diesel-soaked industrial area, with its tire shops, fuel station, construction yards, and the small port itself, an all-business concern, not a pleasure boat in sight.

Not wanting to arrive at camp empty-handed, we decided to check out the local pizza restaurant.

It was like any college town pizza joint back home: rough paneled walls and wooden tables, familiar smells, beer bottles, a dartboard. A bearded guy behind the counter manned the busy ovens beneath an oversized menu listing the various combinations; stacks of cardboard to-go cartons were piled everywhere.

I was surprised to hear the customers speaking Spanish, so complete was the familiarity of the ambience. We ordered a carne especial and a half-dozen large pizzas to go. There is something comforting about finding oneself in a familiar zone after being in a foreign place for a while, however temporary it may be, and that pizza parlor in Puerto Madryn had that effect on me. A brief rest stop.

But we were soon back on the road, well-fed, boxed pizzas and a case of orange sodas in the back, map in hand, heading for our new home. We soon turned off the pavement at a hand-lettered sign, per the map's instructions, and started down a dusty track. We were obviously on someone's ranch land, wild-looking cattle were unexpectedly popping up out of the brush periodically, and we had to pass through several gates.

These gates were something new to me, not hinged gates, but sections of the fence that could be detached from their wire loops and dragged aside to let the traffic pass, then reattached. Our instructions from Roger were specific about the urgent necessity to close all the gates behind us, for obvious reasons. We were determined that cetacean research was not about to be set back twenty years because Roger was kicked out of his camp as a result of an escapee Argentine cattle herd. Not on our watch. We were determined to master the gates.

The latch was a simple but ingenious arrangement that consisted of a wire loop at the bottom for the detachable gate post bottom to rest in and a stick on a wire from the other post used to lever the gate over and then secure the top. Much easier to use than to describe, it soon became a timed competition event for the designated "gateador" to leap out, open the gate, drag it aside, wave the car through, reattach the gate, and leap back in the still-moving car. But that foolishness came later. For now, we were fastidious about our gate technique.

It was just getting dark when we at last topped a rise and saw the lights of camp below. A big fire was burning in a central fire pit, a kitchen lean-to was set up near it, a small camp trailer was off to one side, and an inflatable boat, a couple of cars (one Falcon), and several tents were scattered about. You could just make out the beach and the water of the gulf a short distance from camp. It looked great.

We made our way down the dirt track and rolled into camp amid great fanfare, long lost halloos from Roger, and introductions all around. There was a fellow American researcher, Vicki Roundtree, who was studying whale lice (her subsequent paper was to be called "The Louse That Moored," possibly the only humorously-titled research paper ever produced), several Argentine grad students, and novelist Cormac McCarthy, whom Roger had met when they both were awarded MacArthur grants. He was down in Patagonia researching the area for a new book and had stopped by for a few weeks on his way to Tierra del Fuego. The camp cook, and diver, and all-around capable guy Carlos Garcia was behind the lean-to grilling his signature asado chimichurri steaks, and there was the largest jug of wine I had ever seen in my life resting near one of the seating logs by the fire. It was encased in a woven wicker basket with a handle on either side, obviously a two-man job to carry around. A good sign. It had all the appearances of a happy camp.

More steaks were put on the grill, our pizzas were relegated to the ice box for the moment (not that they weren't appreciated, cold pizza and orange soda were later to become a lunch tradition), and we, large plastic water glasses of wine from the giant jug in hand, were arranged around the fire for some catching up. It was a great night, culminating after dinner with the entire camp reeling around in the brush making a group decision on the most ideal tent sites for the new guests. After much deliberation on the merits of higher (harder), well-drained sites vs. lower (softer), sandy areas, relative views, and proximity to latrine areas, etc., and amid much well-meaning advice, Flip and I both staked out our respective territories, erected our new-fangled tents, drug our outfits from the car, and gratefully flopped down in our new homes to finally sleep.

In a Magic Land

The scene that greeted me upon awakening the next morning made one of those indelible mental snapshots that stay with you for a lifetime. The sun was just illuminating the gulf around whose calm surface were arranged a half-dozen or so huge inert whale tails, flukes calmly pointing straight up, the whales resting head down, bobbing and sailing gently around in the bay. I'd never seen anything like it; it looked like some whale-tail-sculpture art exhibit. As the sun broke onto the beach, I saw a pair of brown and white wild guanacos galloping madly alongside this scene, apparently for the sheer joy of it, which would turn out to be their daily routine. Rheas, large flightless birds, were darting around in the brush. What was this place?

The camp was stirring. Carlos was making the incredibly strong coffee he somehow produced every morning by filtering the brew (I think this was the procedure, I couldn't pin him down) through one of his socks. It was a beautiful day, the conditions were ideal, and we were all anxious to take to the water.

After a hurried breakfast, we gathered cameras and dive gear, pulled on dry suits and weight belts, and manhandled the inflatable boat through the surf, Carlos at the helm, and motored off into the morning. These were Southern Right Whales, up to forty feet long and weighing up to forty tons, floating placidly upside down. I couldn't believe what I was seeing. We coasted up near one of them, slid into the water, and swam right next to the inverted monster, eyeball to eyeball. He eventually righted himself and finned languidly away, but obviously wasn't distressed by our presence.

This was the beginning of a few of the most idyllic weeks of my life. As the days rolled by, we fell into the camp routine of long days on the water with the whales when the weather conditions were good, doing camp chores, tracking whale movements from the observation shack up on the hilltop, or going to town for supplies (including pizzas and more giant wine jugs) when the wind picked up. My lost luggage miraculously appeared at the bus station, along with Dr. Jim Darling, who had come down to join us, and who was to write the story for the magazine. The incredible intimate whale encounters continued. The whales had no fear of us, the older whales and mating groups were indifferent, and some of the young whales mildly curious, sometimes lifting our little boat out of the water with their backs, one actually gathering Flip in under its pectoral fin for a scary underwater ride. One mating group ran right over the top of me when I got too close swimming across their path, but not out of any sense of malice I'm sure, they were just preoccupied.

The nights were spent around the fire, and we fell into a routine (Cormac's idea) that should be instituted as a requirement for any future international gathering, probably starting with the U.N. After the usual exquisite asado steak dinner and glasses of wine, we would begin a round of bi-lingual joke telling that inevitably degenerated into an uproarious Babel, with people weeping helplessly with laughter and falling backward off their logs. The procedure went like this: First, a Spanish speaker would begin a joke, stopping every few moments for the story to be translated for the benefit of the English speakers. Next, it was an English speaker's turn, with translations into Spanish. Some strange, unintended, and wonderful twist would inevitably be introduced in the translation, and the tales spun increasingly out of control into some other realm of communication.

The days rolled by, and the southern spring advanced with the appearance of thousands of tiny yellow flowers popping up amid the brush. The exposed film canisters were beginning to outnumber the unused ones, and then one morning it happened.

Several of us were standing on the beach trying to gauge the weather conditions when a lone figure on horseback appeared in the distance. As he got closer, I realized that it was a gaucho. The flat brimmed hat, the stocky saddle, the cropped horse tail, the whole bit. We stood in awed silence as the figure approached. To us guys he gave only a curt nod. Looking at Vicki, he touched his hat brim and spoke: "Hola, chica." That was it. It was perfect. He continued on, and we stared dumbly after.

It was as if the appearance of the gaucho had added the only piece that had been missing from the whole. It was suddenly clear our sojourn here in Patagonia was almost over. There were a few more loose ends to tidy up, a couple of general people and camp shots to take, equipment cases to pack, and good-byes and addresses to exchange, but it now had a bittersweet air of finality. It had been wonderful, but the job was now finished. It was time to go.

Two Parties

Ending and Beginnings

The following accounts are relevant to this collection because they involve events that led ultimately to that first trip to Maui where I was to initially meet Flip and the gang, and then much later to events that transpired to lead me back again to Hawaii.

These events were parties, actually. Two bookend fiascos, which occurred many years apart. But both surprising in their development and intensity and both coincidentally ending in spectacular fires.

Party One

Country of Origin

My friend Carter and I had scored these incredible summer jobs during our college years. We were river guides on the Rogue River in southern Oregon, taking clients on week-long guided trips through the white water wilderness, rowing bouncy inflatable rubber rafts down the river during the day and stopping to make camp at night. It was really a magical time, and a great deal of fun for us as well as (I assume) for the guests.

But looking back on it I'm afraid we may have de-evolved a bit toward a more primitive life form during those hot summer months as those seasons wore on. For example our sole article of summer clothing was a single pair of ragged cut-off jeans, (it seemed to be an unwritten rule among the boatmen that there could be no replacing these once the season had started), repaired haphazardly as necessary with duct tape, with a predictable scabrous-looking result. We even eventually totally dispensed with wearing anything else at all, including shirts and shoes, our feet developing thick horny soles from scampering over sharp and searing rocks carrying bags and gear to and from the rafts when we stopped to make camp, every square inch of our unprotected skin burned and re-burned by the summer sun. If anyone had needed some Bushmen extras in a Kalahari movie we were their guys.

And mentally we may have shown some signs of degeneration as well. For example, at one point the parent raft company encouraged us to name our rafts, even sent us the silver paint to write the names on the front, and sent us some pictures of examples others in the company had used elsewhere on other rivers. There was the raft *Zippity-Doo-Dah* from the Colorado River bunch, and one named *John Muir* from the California contingent, written in bold letters across the black rubber. We thought naming the crafts was a fine idea.

Being of a certain age and maturity level, I named my boat the *Quivering Thigh*, and painted it large. I can't remember what Carter named his, but it was something equally sordid. I do remember a few raised eyebrows from the more genteel guests as they climbed aboard at the beginning of the trips when they registered those names. I even remember one mother and daughter group actually changing rafts in alarm when they saw the name on my boat. Most people reacted with a resigned sort of shock when they realized that the shaggy creatures before them on the riverbank were not only going on the trip with them, but were also to be their guides. But of course that was before they got to know and love us for the wholesome fun-loving people we actually were, despite initial appearances. Or maybe it was a matter of the clients identifying with their captors Stockholm-syndrome-like when they realized that there was no way out of the wilderness other than continuing down the river with the likes of us after they climbed aboard. But no matter, regardless of how the trip began, we always seemed to turn into a convivial group as the trip wore on. But for now, back to that first party.

The New Back Forty

These expeditions occupied us about eight or nine days each trip, between the breaking down of the gear and the transport, and there were two or three scheduled each month, so that left us some time off between trips to rest and recover. And to get into more mischief as it turned out.

Some friends of ours had become caretakers of an old farmstead up near where our river put-in spot was located, a place the former owners had named *Back Forty*, which was in need of caretaking and fixing up, and that became our headquarters when we weren't on the river. Unfortunately the main house had burned down some time ago, so all that remained were the fields, and some barns and outbuildings. But there was a fine big grassy central area in the center of the property next to the main barn and a creek where we set about building a huge fire pit. We surrounded the central fire area with comfortable furniture, big stuffed couches and chairs and things, and since there were lots of convenient trees for stringing hammocks in strategic spots by the creek in view of the fire we put in lots of those as well. It was heaven really, a perfect summer hideaway for outdoor living and sleeping under the stars.

We had gotten into the habit in those long summers of hosting big gatherings on Saturday nights during our time off between the river trips at our new place. We would pull a big old flatbed truck that was on the farm up near the central area and use it as a stage. It seemed everybody played guitar in those days, or drums, or something. I remember some approximation of music being produced constantly.

These gatherings were great fun, and became legendary, the groups getting a little larger each time we had an event, crowds coming from miles away and reeling around in various stages of various intoxications in the firelight, laughter echoing through in the trees. It was so much fun, of course it couldn't last.

At first we knew everybody at these things, but as the crowds got larger at subsequent parties I guess we lost control of our guest list. There were lots of girls at these events, naturally, and we began to notice some faces we hadn't seen before.

It turned out, unbeknownst to us, that one of our nearest neighbors out there in the wilderness was a compound called the *Country School for Wayward High School Girls*, a place established out there in the boonies that boarded troubled girls from the city, the idea being that some fresh air and the simple country life were just the ticket for setting straying urban waifs back on the proper path. The unfortunate proximity of that school may have been our downfall.

Bad Fences Make Frisky Neighbors

One afternoon toward the end of that last summer our friend Frank, the local sheriff, a good guy whom we'd come to know socially, stopped by with some grave news. It seems there had been some complaints from a neighbor, (he couldn't say who), not only about the traffic and noise from our gatherings, (even though we were miles from anyone), but there was also the more serious rumors of the possibility of underage drinking taking place. Apparently there were suspicions that some of the wayward girls had been sneaking away at night to our functions, which could well have been true, they may have had a point. These citizens weren't going to stand for it anymore and Frank was tasked with setting up a raid the next time a party took place. This looked like the end of a grand time, but we'd finally finished college and summer was winding down anyway, so it was probably time for a change.

This was a pretty serious accusation, and we didn't want any part of it. So we reluctantly put out the word that there was to be no party this Saturday, in fact probably no more parties at the *Back Forty* at all, and we set about cleaning up the place to prepare for our impending visitors.

We began tidying up the place, hauling off empty bottles and sweeping the ground smooth. We fashioned a huge sign that read "WE'RE CLEAN FRANK!" and hung it on the barn, and we tacked dozens of *WE DO NOT SERVE MINORS* plastic signs we had gotten from the local beer distributor on the trees leading up the dirt drive to the place.

Satisfied that we were as ready as we would ever be, that Saturday morning dawned clear and calm and peaceful, and we awoke refreshed with the clear consciences of good intentions, relieved really to be acting in the public good for a change. We were even quite polite to each other for the moment, none of the

59

usual unkind razzing remarks that made up the bulk of our normal daily exchanges, there was a certain smug civility in the air, the superiority of the recently morally uplifted. It wouldn't last, of course, but it started out as a civilized morning.

We puttered around the place most of the day, arranging and tidying up; the place had never looked so good. In the early afternoon an old friend of ours, a guy named Smiley, and a few of his musician friends showed up with their instruments planning to play that night, not having gotten the word that the party had been canceled. But no worries, we explained to them about the upcoming raid, and the need for them to be on their best behavior if they wanted to stay.

Electric Jug Band

So we settled in around the fire pit for some quiet guitar and conversation, and a big jug of wine they had brought began making the rounds, no harm in that we thought. Our first mistake as it turned out.

There was some suspicion later that their wine jug contained something in addition to just wine, judging how quickly events overtook us, (and knowing musicians in general), but that is just speculation. It may have been that in our unaccustomed clean slate of innocence that our defenses were down.

When the second and third groups arrived later, within minutes of each other, alarm bells should have gone off, but in our mellow newfound state of grace, (and probably nudged along by whatever was dissolved in that wine), we of course welcomed the newcomers. Another stern warning about being on our best behavior because of the upcoming raid was of course administered to the newcomers, with solemn wide-eyed promises from them to do just that of course offered earnestly up, and all was in harmony, just a quiet gathering of young citizens enjoying a summer eve.

Of course more bottles and a few discreet joints made regular rounds and I am afraid we began to lose control of the evening remarkably quickly. First of all there was an unexpected panic when some of the group heard more cars coming up the drive, the old doper paranoia instinct kicking in uncontrollably in a certain number of guests. There was some dashing to the woods, some stashing of stashes, and a few "Cheese it, the Cops" kind of Keystone reflexes. But we managed to calm the group, this was just our friend Frank the Sheriff who was going to be dropping by after all, and it turned out it wasn't the cops driving in anyway, just our crazy friends Rusty and Susie and pals who had brought along a big box of fireworks, among other things, in hopes of enlivening the evening. We gathered everyone back together around the fire pit, repeated our warnings about good behavior, (likely a somewhat less focused entreaty I fear, with something like the first smell of overheating brakes on an overloaded big rig headed down a steep grade seeming to waft up from the fire…).

But it all seemed contained at this point, we even started up the little generator for the band, some soothing music seemed like just the ticket at a time like this. (Probably not the best plan. In retrospect our judgment may have been a trifle skewed about now, who knew what was in that wine jug?)

Seconds Anyone?

It was probably about this time that we totally lost control of the party, although we didn't realize it, we thought we were still containing things well. More headlights were continually coming up the drive, and we would try to greet each new group of guests with the

61

admonition to be on their best behavior, (Frank was coming!), and we of course received solemn promises that they would do that before they joined the dancing throng. But we couldn't keep up with all of the new arrivals. Strange people kept appearing; some youngish looking girls we didn't recognize were traipsing in and out of the firelight. In truth, as the arcs of these things go, we were no longer having a party, the party was having us.

Things were really percolating along at this point unfortunately, it looked remarkably like a typical Saturday night at the Back Forty, singing and dancing and drum circles spontaneously springing up accompanying Smiley and the band, couples hooking up and wandering into the trees. A rare minor argument broke out at some point between a couple of old friends, some inconsequential matter, (actually these gatherings were normally amazingly devoid of tension, as befitting the times).

But these guys couldn't come to an agreement about something or other, and it was determined that some conflict resolution intervention was in order. It was decided that a duel was the only answer. A duel using a couple of Roman Candles from the big fireworks box. Proper procedure was put in place. Someone found some welding gloves for holding the weapons, a couple of pairs of dusty safety goggles and an old work glove were unearthed from the barn for one combatant to slap the other with while proclaiming "By God I am provoked! My seconds will call upon you forthwith!" Seconds were put into place, a dueling field was identified, and the thing commenced. Of course everyone, including the band, had to see this, an appreciative raucous crowd gathered, there was quite a spectator gallery at the dueling field while the combatants lined up back to back for their obligatory ten paces, their seconds standing by with lit matches to light the candles for the turn and fire sequence. It started as quite a civilized affair, (I had to suppose, I didn't really have anything to compare it to really, never having been to an actual duel before.) But decorum was observed, the principals walked off their paces on the mark, nobody panicked and turned and fired early, the candles were calmly lit as the paces were completed.

But then all hell broke loose.

Roman Candles when ignited at close range put out a staggering amount of smoke and fire, fiery missiles were caroming at first off the duelists, then as they dodged and lurched around in the conflagration, off the trees, into the sky, ricocheting off the ground, the spectators, everywhere. And then of course some miscreant had the bright idea of throwing the whole fireworks box into the bonfire. The resulting sound and fury was mind-numbing, explosions and countless fireballs were whizzing by everywhere through the smoke.

And then of course right about then Frank and the posse showed up. Two cop cars appeared with lights flashing through the fire and fog, Armageddon was here. Complete panic gripped the crowd and they fled in every direction, galloping through the fields and splashing through the creek, a full rout was in progress within seconds.

I'm not proud of this, but my brain stem apparently took charge at this point and I fled mindlessly into a field. Glancing back I could just make out several uniformed deputies through the smoke and fireballs emerging from their cars and looking up in confusion at the big "WE"RE CLEAN FRANK!" sign on the barn illuminated by the explosions. I heard running footsteps behind me, spurring me onto a frantic dash, full flight, the survival portion of my limbic brain in total control now, my brain screaming RUN RUN. Legs churning and heart pounding, incredibly I still heard running footfalls behind me, my arms started to windmill as I leaned forward, they were gonna git me! I tried to zig and then zag into the darkness, but I couldn't shake the pursuit. I turned to face the inevitable and Carter ran smack into me, knocking us both to the ground.

"Jesus!" he said, both of our breaths now coming in hoarse gasps. "I didn't think I was ever gonna catch you!"

When we had recovered sufficiently to move, we crawled over behind the protection of a low hill and made our way over to a vantage point where we could look down onto our recently abandoned fire pit.

The explosions seemed to have slowed, only the occasional surprised tardy firecracker now, deputies were fanned out with flashlights light-sabering through the smoke, and we could hear lots of splashing and girlish giggling coming from the creek and among the trees as partygoers fled into parts unknown.

Exitstential Strategies

Of course the proper thing to do at this point would have been to march back down to find Frank and hope to find some small mercy. But it was odd. It seemed that the scene below us was far removed from our comfortable perch somehow; something detached unfolding before us, with a life of its own and an infinite branching of possibilities. What was in that wine jug anyway? I guess if unsophisticated rural youth can be permitted to experience an existential moment this was it. We had a glimpse of the howling void, the capriciousness of existence, the future untethered. A many-forked path. At any rate a change was definitely in the offing, a chapter was closing. But if one chapter was closing that meant another was opening. We stayed put and idly began to make plans, most involving removing ourselves to a place far away. This was when Carter first raised the possibility of searching out a long lost cousin reportedly living in Hawaii, and that struck us both as a brilliant idea.

There was certainly a bit of music to be faced here of course, but it really wasn't as bad as we feared. No apprehensions were made that night; the fleeing crowd stayed just out of the reach of the pursuing flashlights, most of the crowd knew the terrain pretty well and slipped away into the night. It was a good thing Sheriff Frank was a friend of ours, things could certainly have been much worse. Apparently satisfied that they had discharged their duty, the party was over, the invading force withdrew and a much more subdued group coalesced out of the darkness to gather around the fire. Everyone knew, as Jackson Browne sang about that time, that all good things have to come to an end. Fun as the summer at the *Back Forty* had been, it was over.

Party Two
Party of the Second Part

The second bookend party of this set occurred some years later, after my first stint in Hawaii (we did indeed follow through with our escape plan), then subsequent foray into the cruise ship world. This one took place in Alaska.

The cruise ship company I worked for had branched out into the idea of getting into the day boat business, involving boats designed not for their normal multiple-day overnight cruising but for taking larger groups of people on shorter day long excursions and adventures in some of the areas we operated. They had commissioned our friends at Nichols Brothers Boats to build them a fast 300 passenger catamaran type ferry outfitted to take guests on day sightseeing trips around southeast Alaska during the summer season, with the idea of positioning the boat to Hawaii for the winter months for cruising there. An exciting prospect to be sure and I eagerly joined the project.

Sue Me Tsunami

Of course the vessel construction was behind schedule, as these things always go, and it was midsummer before the new boat was finally completed and ready to head north, so we were feeling some pressure to get the craft up to Juneau as soon as possible to begin our season. The trip north went well, we made good time, as the boat was fast, 25 knots or so. We arrive at the channel to Juneau around mid-morning on a beautiful early July day, making what we thought was an impressive entry to town, slowing down at the last minute to execute a Captain Ron landing at the town wharf, a smug and happy crew. What we hadn't realized was that the big crowd on the beach we had passed on the way into town was the annual city 4th of July bash highlighted by the beloved traditional sand castle building contest. I still have a copy of the following day's newspaper bearing the headline: *"Tour Boat Mars Fourth of July Celebration!"*. Apparently our wake had hit the beach just before the sand castle judging was to take place, the huge wave engulfing the sand constructions, picnic baskets, blanketed families, then sweeping the beach clean as it ebbed and retreated. A disgusted citizen described the scene to me later; children crying, adults cursing. All in all it was a less than stellar entrance on our part. It was some weeks before anyone in town would even talk to us. I am surprised we weren't badly beaten.

Chastened, we began our tour program, running tourists over to Glacier Bay during the day and taking cruise ship passengers into Tracy Arm in the evening. It was turning into a success, and gradually the townsfolk softened to the point that we didn't fear for our lives when we went into town.

What about Bob?

A few weeks into the program our engineer had a family emergency and had to fly back home so we were in dire need of a qualified mechanical guy, these new high power engines and systems needed constant attention and a steady hand looking after them. We had hired a local guy as a bartender who told us he had a friend who lived in a tent near him outside of town who was a sort of mechanical genius, somebody who called himself "Noodles" and had come up from California for the fishing. He could arrange for him to come interview. It couldn't hurt, I thought, it would take some time to locate and fly in an engineer from home, but frankly I thought the possibility of actually finding a qualified guy living in a tent just outside of Juneau was remote at best, but I told the bartender to bring his friend around in any case, and then pretty much forgot about it.

But when we came into the dock the next day there was this bearded scruffy-looking character waiting for us on the pier; Noodles himself as it turned out. After the passengers had been unloaded he came aboard and introduced himself. His real name was Bob Dippold and he was indeed a character. An endless stream of jokes and puns were issuing from this guy, so much for his taciturn hermit appearance, and it turned out he really did know what he was talking about. He was familiar with these engines, despite the fact that they were a new model; he had worked on similar ones on a previous boat he had been on. In touring the engine room he had a lot of system improvement suggestions, and they made a lot of sense. He was hired immediately, finding a qualified engineer who was also funny and good company was an almost unheard-of irresistible combination, and it turned out we became fast friends and worked together and had countless adventures in the years to come. But back to that party.

The company had found us a house to live in for the summer, a great little place close to town. The only fly in the ointment being that it was overseen by this horrible creature by the name of Katherine Krabtree the company had hired to manage the Juneau office, a little hard-bitten pitbull of a woman who mysteriously had an inflated sense of self. (She always referred to herself as the "Alaska Regional Manager", her self imposed title, which she would shoehorn into every conversation with a haughty air as she charged about. One of her more endearing aspects was her habit of getting bombed at every company function, loudly berating everyone in sight and announcing her resignation, then showing up the next day for work having completely forgotten the whole performance. Impressive actually.) She took it upon herself to let herself into our house during the day while we were working to check on things and to see that things were tidy and perfect. (And incredibly to look for evidence that we might be bringing girls over, which she apparently frowned upon. I remember once she found a stray hairpin and raised quite a fuss, we couldn't believe it.) We didn't pay her much mind, but I mention it only to put in context what her reaction must have been to the events that transpired later.

Our season was a great success, we were very proud of the way the project had gone, but inevitably our time here was winding down and it was time to begin thinking about heading out and repositioning the boat to Hawaii for the winter season.

Hawaii Heave-Ho

It was Dippold, of course, who had the bright idea of staging a going-away party, a Hawaiian luau, to say goodbye to all of our new friends and to give closure to our season. But it grew in scale, as these things happen, as we got caught up in the planning. Our guest list seemed somewhat paltry in looking at it; we had only been in town for a couple of months after all. So Bob had some handbills printed up announcing our luau, inviting Juneauites to stop by in their best Hawaiian garb, (he listed the party time as *"7 pm until the police come"*, he thought that was funny), and he tacked them up around town, thinking we might round out our gathering.

He really put some effort into this shindig, he bought a whole pig from the local butcher, and proceeded to dig a hole in the back yard in which to cook it. The pig's head he saved to make an elaborate centerpiece; the night of the grand party he stuck an apple in its mouth and surrounded it with flowers and Hawaiian snacks and put it on a big table next to the punch bowl by the barbeque out back. We had some Hawaiian posters we had found and as many fresh flowers as we could find strewn about, the place was really looking festive when the appointed time came around and partygoers began arriving.

Who would have thought a little Alaskan town would contain that many aloha shirts, grass skirts and coconut bras? This was turning into quite a gathering, Captain Cook would have been impressed and felt right at home. (On his first trip to Hawaii, not the second one when he unexpectedly came back and they killed him, realizing he wasn't the god Lono after all. Good lesson that; when you manage to make a grand exit stay gone.)

What a grand time this was turning out to be, it seems Alaskans really love a good party and we were making lots of new friends, we all wished we had done this earlier, (but maybe it was better suited to a final act as things turned out…).

Just when we thought things couldn't get any more manic, Hawaiian music blaring and impromptu hulas breaking out among the surging throng, another colorful group would stage a grand entrance, all decked out in South Seas finery and doing their best impression of a crazed Polynesian invasion force.

Porcine Prayerfest, or Pighiel!

We never did find out who did it, or exactly when, but at some point in the festivities the pig's head Dippold had arranged as a centerpiece got placed on the barbeque.

Now I had never suspected what could ultimately happen to a pig's head when superheated, but it is a truly impressive spectacle. The thing suddenly exploded into flame, fiery jets streaming from eye sockets, nostrils and ears. It made a sound like a V1 rocket engine on a test bed, sending a pillar of flame ten feet into the air and lighting up the whole back yard and everything in it.

Everyone froze. The music stopped and in a sort of unified trance first one and then all the rest of the partygoers fell to their knees and began to bow to the apparition. Maybe it stirred some sort of Jungian collective unconscious reaction, (more likely it was just

70

ridiculous good fun), but for whatever reason the whole party arranged themselves around the fiery thing, the eye sockets sending burning jets of benediction, or something, out over the supplicated crowd while spontaneous chanting and bowing suffused the worshipers, an incredible spectacle I will never forget, like a scene from Dante or Tolkien.

Of course that was when the police showed up. There were several of them, they marched in initially with what I assume was righteous authority determined to put an end to this noisy affront, but confusion quickly overcame them and they simply stopped and stared in non-comprehension at the scene before their eyes. I doubt this sort of thing happened often in Juneau.

For several seconds there was no sound but the crackling of the burning pig's head. The chanting had stopped when the police arrived and now the two groups simply stared at each other.

The spell had been broken. Many of the partygoers surreptitiously slipped away, others began gathering up their things, and some exchanged subdued greetings with the officers, whom they apparently knew, this being a small town. A fire extinguisher was deployed on the burning head, and the whole event deflated and dispersed. A noise infraction warning was issued, but obviously it was just a formality at this point, the party was over.

After the cops and the partygoers had left we sat amid the ruins in a sort of stupor. What a party. We were exhausted. We did some cursory tidying up but decided to tackle the rest of the cleanup after a few hours sleep.

A misguided idea of course. The next morning dawned through a miasma of rum punch fumes and the reeking effluvia of the still-smoking blackened pig skull on the barbeque. We made a cursory gathering of sticky cups and crushed flower leis, took down posters and swept up shrimp tails and crushed macadamia nuts, but after an hour or so of cleaning up we realized we were out of time. We had to get to our boat to start south, we had a tide to catch, and that waits, as the saying goes, for no man, including the sorry likes of us. At some point we realized we probably weren't going to get our cleaning deposit back, especially with that thing on the barbeque, and that we probably had the further consequence of our friend Katherine being put out with us. But we hadn't expected such a tumultuous event. Circumstances had conspired against us, as Cormac would say.

I took one last look at that scorched smoking skull as we were leaving and thought I detected in its blackened face a faint expression of reproach, even from it, and a whiff of that familiar existential feeling of doors randomly opening and closing, of capricious paths, wafted over to me. Or maybe it was just a whiff of burnt pork. In any case we were sailing off to Hawaii. Perhaps we could find shelter from the sins of our excesses in a sacred City of Refuge. But there was no mistake; another chapter was definitely closed.

Harbor Rats and Humpbacks- The Early Days

Throw me in the Briar Patch

Imagine going back in time a few decades and looking down from some great height on the Hawaiian Islands. If you focused in on that strange-looking double island, Maui, and concentrated on the northwestern shore of the westernmost island, you would be able to make out a crumbling seaside town, with a prominent old lighthouse at the entrance to a small harbor, just offshore of a huge banyan tree. If you looked more closely at the harbor, you would see a swarm of activity, tour boats coming and going and a colorful tide of aloha-shirted tourists surging up and down the waterfront. A step closer and you might see the old raggedy homeless guy the kids called *"Maki* (meaning dead) *Cow"* (for the way he smelled), climbing out of the dumpster by the dinghy dock, and a drug deal being consummated across the wall at the south end of the harbor. That's probably too close, so we'll back off a bit.

Lahaina Harbor, that beautiful U-shaped old breakwater harbor at the base of the green West Maui mountains, was to become the center of the fledgling

Hawaii whale-research universe. It was (and still is) a singular place. With profuse apologies to John Steinbeck, his well-used description of Monterey's Cannery Row as "a poem, a stink, a grating noise, a quality of light..." somehow evokes for me the old harbor as it was back then much better than anything else I can imagine— light, stink, and all. In this case, the grating noise was generally coming from the trunk of some unfortunate tourist's parked rental car as it was being pried open by some local kids so they could steal whatever was left inside. The only other feeling I could add to that list would be the vague sense of free-floating menace that emanated from the Lair of the Black Coral Divers at the far end of the harbor, but more about that later.

It is worth relating how some of us ended up being there at that time. My journey started like this:

My friend Carter and I, on a whim one smoke-filled evening in Oregon, decided to buy these one-way plane tickets to Hawaii, a place we'd never been, but which sounded insanely attractive in a brochure we'd found. We had finally finished college and had the last of our summer river-guiding job money, and were in that sobering, sudden vacuum of time after an endless lifetime-to-date of schooling. It was that familiar clueless-kid-confronts-world phase.

We had just enough money to get there, and not enough sense to worry about much beyond that.

We ended up choosing to go to Maui on the strength of looking for a possible remote cousin of Carter's who may or may not have been living there. We never located the cousin, but did manage shortly after we arrived to stake out a private camping spot on a remote beach in a thorny *kiawe* brush thicket on the sparsely populated windward side of the island. Nobody knew we were there, hiding in our thicket. We would see occasional groups of surfers a distance down the coast, but we were left alone. The sum total of our camping gear consisted of a couple of hammocks, a Swiss Army knife, some cooking pots and water jugs, diving masks and fins, and a big roll of rubber surgical tubing we figured would be useful for making the fishing sling spears and slingshots we would need to catch our food.

As newly arrived savages, we set about carving up the local *kiawe* branches and fabricating our weapons, and happily inhabiting Paradise. After some trial and error, we soon learned to spear the reef fish in front of our camp and became such deadly slingshot masters that no black rock crab was safe sunning itself within a fifty-yard radius of our little settlement.

Everything went into the cooking pot, along with the little cone-shaped rock-hugging limpets called *opihi* in Hawaiian, which we learned the local Japanese fish market down the road would pay us top dollar for, and the gathering of which became our main source of income, along with the round *puka* shells we collected and sold to the local jewelry stores. The money from these amusements kept us in rice and condiments to go along with our seafood, as well as financing the setting up of our fermenting buckets and straining gear to make the strange-tasting but effective guava wine we made from the fruit of the nearby guava trees.

We were in deadbeat-kid heaven. Our corporeal needs taken care of by our never-ending supply of seafood, and our spiritual needs addressed by the guava wine and the mushrooms that grew in a cow pasture nearby, we were surprisingly content. So content, in fact, that idle time presented itself (always the barometer of a successful culture). So, naturally, we turned our attention toward the domestication of neighboring animal species, a logical human cultural progression; in this case, we focused on the mongooses we could occasionally see streaking through our camp. Endless hours were spent fabricating a complex, humane mongoose trap, punctuated by occasional trips to the mushroom field for more inspiration. Carter had tamed a pet raccoon as a kid, who used to ride around on his shoulder, and we saw no reason why we shouldn't soon be sporting pet mongooses around. And knowing how girls love cute animals, the chance to use them as romantic props figured into our plan as well, as soon as we got the chance to meet any girls.

We were proud of our mongoose trap. It was a thing of beauty, composed of a woven cage with intricately carved little levers, latches, and rubber tubing springs and gates. It was ultimately a great success, as far as capturing mongooses went, but, despite hours of effort, we couldn't seem to win the affection of the little brutes. In fact, we couldn't seem to progress past the stage of having the nasty little red-eyed beasties ferociously flinging themselves at the bars of our cage, snapping and snarling, gnashing their little needle-sharp teeth, and trying not to get away (as you might suppose most gentle woodland creatures would do), but trying their best to get *at* us. We thought maybe we had just managed to catch a few grumpy ones at first, but it turned out they were *all* like that. It was truly frightening. We were grateful they weren't any bigger; we would never have been able to fall asleep out there in the brush again.

But, ultimately we had to give up our mongoose-taming project, not for a lack of trying, and also had to give up our thorny Paradise. We had Eden but no Eves.

It was the quest for feminine companionship that finally forced us into society. It seemed that meeting Maui girls required money. And a permanent address wouldn't hurt.

Slouching toward Lahaina

We reluctantly made our way down the coast to the outskirts of Lahaina in response to a Help Wanted ad put in the local paper by a big industrial laundry that was set up in an old former pineapple cannery site. This place was huge; they did all of the linens and laundry for the big hotels. It was a cavernous warehouse full of giant washers and dryers and big folding machines, steam pipes and chutes running in all directions back into the darkness. We presented our unkempt selves to the head office. To our amazement, we were hired on immediately. I was the new assistant operations manager and Carter was the new assistant supply manager. Apparently there was a labor shortage.

We had no idea what we were doing, but that didn't seem to be a problem. My supervisor was a diminutive Filipino guy named Barney who assigned me my tool belt and sent me out into the bowels of the laundry whenever some big machine hiccupped. I figured it was only a matter of time before I was found out as a fraud and fired, but I kept finding ways to keep the contraptions clanking along.

Working there was a cultural education as well. As an example, Barney announced to us all at lunch one day that where he came from, if any man compromised another man's wife it was the aggrieved man's responsibility to kill and eat the other man. *Kill and eat?* Carter and I exchanged wide-eyed looks. Where was it exactly that he came from? He may have been only toying with us new *haole* guys, but it got our attention; we

77

made sure we knew which girl was his wife and maintained a healthy distance. (Not that hard to do, actually, thinking back on it, his beloved looked a little like Manuel Noriega in drag).

Another challenge was that the local Hawaiian and Filipino and Portuguese workers all spoke the local pidgin English, and that took some getting used to...for example: *"Hey brah, you not so akami or wat? Hannova da kine screwdriver!"* would translate roughly to "Please pass me a screwdriver, moron." But the communication was always made clear, usually accompanied by threatening gestures.

Finally armed with our first paychecks, real money, we were able to rent a little apartment and start our foray into Lahaina society. We took to having a beer after work at the Pioneer Inn by the harbor. The first time I looked out toward the water I was smitten by the whole harbor scene.

Boats were continuously coming and going: sail boats, dive boats, and big tourist party boats, (no whale-watching boats back then, it really hadn't quite caught on yet). But what fascinated me were the sport fishing boats. I thought this was the epitome of cool. The fishing boat captains seemed to be another race entirely, sitting up high in their flying bridge thrones and wearing a look of superior nonchalance (it turned out it was really a look of vacant mindlessness, but I didn't know that until later). They would roar their big boats into the harbor, casually wheel them around, then gun the engines as they maneuvered into the slips, flying the flags of the fish they had caught...the deckhands would casually flip the lines onto cleats and haul big fish up to the scales to be weighed...it was incredible. I wanted to do that.

But it turned out every other deadbeat transplant newly arrived on Maui and desperately trying to learn to speak pidgin wanted to do that, too; it was insanely difficult to get a job anywhere down in the harbor, much less on a fishing boat.

So we continued to toil away down at the laundry, but I was determined to get onto one of those boats somehow. Around this time, Carter had enough of laundry work and decided to leave Maui for a while and head back home, but I didn't want to give up yet. I wanted to be a part of that harbor life, so I stayed on.

And finally it happened. Some weeks later, a girl I had met invited me to a party where some of the fishing crews were in attendance, and I overheard the news that one of the deckhands on a sport fishing boat was quitting. Unbelievable. Give up the greatest job in the world? Insanity. Oh well, not for me to figure. But getting the job wasn't going to be that easy.

Harboring Hopes

It turned out there were at least a dozen candidates for the deckhand position, many of them there at the party. There was no time to lose. I quickly cornered the captain at the beer keg, a young guy not much older than me, and made my pitch. I'd been river guiding (I told him), so I knew how to handle lines and knots, and I threw in a few exaggerations about my boating skills in general and basically made such a pest of myself that I got on the tryout list. It turned out that the way this captain planned to fill the open position was to let various hopefuls come out on the boat for a tryout day and see how they performed…I was ecstatic…but terrified that I'd oversold my skills.

The tryout morning finally came. I had taken the day off from the laundry and was down at the boat at dawn, and I was focused, anticipating the every need of the captain and guests, and cleaning everything in sight, all the while keeping up my best approximation of charming banter. In retrospect, I was probably annoying, but I *wanted* this job.

The actual mechanics of the job were straightforward; we were going to be trolling six lines at various lengths, using a variety of big lures and feathers. The deckhand's job was to keep an eye on the lures, monitor the drag set on the reels, and assist in clearing lines, gaffing (snagging the fish with a gaff, or curved hook on a pole), and helping get the fish in the boat when it came up to the surface. It was exciting, even the smaller two or three pound *akus* (beautiful streamlined fish) were unbelievably energetic, flipping and flailing all around the deck. And the larger brilliantly colored fish called *onos* and *mahi-mahis* were awesome when they came aboard. I wasn't to see the indescribable landing of the king of the sportfish, the blue marlin, until some months later, but I saw enough that first day to hook me.

I thought I had acquitted myself well, but as we were cleaning up the boat after the charter, the captain thanked me for coming and said he would let me know his final decision in a few days, after he had interviewed a few more applicants. So it was back to the laundry for me, waiting for word.

Plucked From the Depths or *Saved by the Bill*

A week later, there was a message for me in the office. I had been chosen for the job and could start the next week. The world took on a new light. I was in a sudden state of grace, and the future was a wonderful place of limitless possibilities. I was going to be working on a boat in Lahaina Harbor. I gave my notice at the laundry. Now that I was leaving, I developed a sudden nostalgia for the place.

After all, I hadn't totally embarrassed myself, I had enjoyed the work, and I had, over time, established an easy relationship with the various characters I worked with. And they had in retrospect been generous in teaching me what I needed to know. It had taken some time to be accepted, but as I got to know my co-workers I became aware of the easy-going tolerance and good humor that has developed in multi-ethnic Hawaii, despite the occasional quick violence. It may have had something to do with the benign climate, but, for whatever reason, the local universal hospitality and laid-back good humor is a wonderful thing. But, sudden nostalgia aside, there was no mistaking my excitement over my new prospects.

So, saying goodbye to my friends at the laundry, I began my apprenticeship in the Lahaina Harbor. Early mornings found me carrying bags of ice for the boat fish bins down Front Street, through the warming air and smells of plumeria and overflowed restaurant dumpsters, through water puddles and sticky banyan leaves, down to the harbor and the boats, and the sound of the Pacific breaking on the harbor wall. I loved it.

The harbor society itself was made up of several distinctly different strata. There were the dinner and party boats clustered up toward the north end, then a smattering of sail and dive boats, then mostly the sport fishing boats toward the south end, culminating in the aforementioned black-coral-diver's area. These strata had their own personalities. The dinner and party boat people were mostly well-meaning and friendly folk, going about their business and keeping to their own schedules and cliques, socializing occasionally with the sail and dive boat bunch. The sport-fishing group was an edgier crowd, hard-partiers for the most part, more prone to tattoos and coarse behavior, lots of California beach kids who had come here for the surfing. Then, in a league of their own, were the total crazies, the black coral divers, who kept to themselves. They had come, mostly I think, from prison. Pity the unsuspecting newbie who wandered uninvited into their dock territory. The only comparable sense of menace that came to mind could be experienced by some unfortunate out-of-towner who unknowingly breezes into the neighborhood outlaw biker bar and plunks down on the alpha leader's favorite barstool. It wasn't that anything was *said* necessarily, it was more of a sensation of imminent doom, a subtle odor maybe, usually accompanied by the hair rising up on the back of one's neck. It didn't take long for new arrivals to the harbor to avoid that area and avoid making eye contact with the denizens.

Black Coral, because of its density and luster when polished, had become a favorite with jewelry-makers and commanded a high price. Unfortunately, it grew in deep water, in tree-like structures, usually at depths of over two hundred feet, and was becoming increasingly rare as the shallower areas were harvested, necessitating deeper and deeper dives. The technique these black coral divers used to harvest the coral was to position their small boats over a promising deep underwater canyon; then, armed with an air tank, a small ax or hatchet, and a large rock for weight, they would plunge straight down, sometimes to as much as three hundred feet, quickly hack off a coral tree at the trunk, then drop the rock and rocket to the surface with their prize. It was incredibly dangerous and foolish and flew in the face of all sane diving practices, but it was making

82

them a lot of money. Of course, between the bends and nitrogen narcosis and all of the other hazards inherent in such insane behavior, a few black coral divers disappeared every year, but it gave the surviving ones a certain mystique and a definite go-to-hell attitude. They lived hard and played harder.

Sure enough, shortly after I started working on the boats a black coral diver failed to return to his boat after a dive, and the harbor organized their customary funeral procession, with all of the boats driving slowly along in a line in front of Lahaina, the missing diver's girlfriend in the lead boat, sobbing and tossing flowers and leis into the water, as a moving eulogy was read over the marine radio. A week later the girlfriend got a call from the departed. It turned out he had become disoriented underwater and missed his boat on the way up and floated over to the island of Molokai, where he had spent the time on an epic drunken bender with some new friends he had met there. He had finally sobered up enough to check in, and could she send someone over to pick him up? These guys were definitely a step beyond anything I had encountered and were to be treated with caution.

Meanwhile, I was having a ball working as a deckhand. And the fishing was incredibly exciting. Experiencing a 500-plus pound marlin suddenly exploding from the water right behind your boat is as thrilling a sight as I have ever seen, and the reason you don't see more pictures of that happening is that most people are frozen in slack-jawed amazement, the brain refusing to believe what the eyes are seeing, camera hanging forgotten around the neck.

I had found my niche now; I couldn't imagine not being able to go out on the water every day. It didn't take me long to realize that if being a deckhand was fun, being the captain would be even more fun, so I did some research and set about getting the credentials. It turned out to be simply a matter of documenting my sea time and undergoing tedious testing by the Coast Guard. When I finally had my captain's license in hand, I knew this was something I was going to do for a while. I knew I was lucky to be young and doing something I loved; none of the things I had done before this even came close.

A Slightly Sticky Film

It wasn't long after I had gotten my license that I was fortunate enough to begin working for Tad Luckey running his charter boat Sport Diver. The old Sporty had begun life as a dive boat and had since been converted to sport fishing. It still had lots of open deck area though, so was a favorite of film crews who occasionally came to Maui for various projects.

Word came that an IMAX movie crew was going to charter the boat for a couple of months to make a film about the Humpback whales.

I wasn't sure what to expect. I was going to miss the fishing every day, but I was curious about the whales we saw coming and going in the channels between the islands, and was intrigued by their eerie wailing songs we could hear underwater, and sometimes could even feel vibrating up through the hull of the boat when we stopped.

The appointed day came and the crew arrived, hauling tons of gear, box after box of cables and film and equipment, and two huge cameras used for the big IMAX film stock. One of the cameras we secured to the bow on a stabilized platform for surface shots, and the other, encased in an underwater housing and weighing around 300 pounds, we rigged to a detachable sled so we could quickly deploy and retrieve it from the water as underwater filming opportunities presented themselves. Luckily our deckhand at the time was a large guy we called Bear, who not only resembled his namesake physically, fur and all, but also was incredibly strong. He didn't talk much, but we soon realized, after the first day of pulling that contraption in and out of the boat several times an hour, that there was no way we could have done it without him.

The film crew had been working together for some time, the Maui portion of the film being the last segment of several. They had reached that stage in a relationship that if it were a certain kind of marriage, (we've all seen this), communication would consist primarily of long periods of silence punctuated by episodes of painful pinching and recriminations. All was not in harmony. They had just come off a difficult shoot in the Red Sea, and dispositions were frayed.

The director, (I'll call him Ron Rockson), turned out to be one of those unfortunate souls whose natural abilities don't quite measure up to their grandiose self-image, and although this seldom poses a problem to the afflicted individual, this can make life difficult for those around him.

He didn't let anyone else make any sort of decisions, no matter how minor, possibly because of the well-justified fear that decisions by others could be sounder than his own, and hence make him look bad. Just a theory. Any questions we had were to be directed to Director Ron. Asking anyone else anything brought a rolling of eyes and a thumb jerking in Ron's direction. As I mentioned, they had been working together for some time.

85

It didn't really affect me one way or the other, for all I knew this was the way all of these film crews worked, (fortunately that turned out not to be the case), but it was fascinating to observe.

I noticed there was one guy along who wasn't part of the regular film crew; he was shooting still photos, documenting the making of the film. It turned out to be Flip Nicklin, who would later become one of the world's foremost underwater photographers, on one of his first photography jobs, but he was just another anonymous picture-taker then. But the fact that he wasn't really directly working under Ron gave him a certain independence, and opportunities for humorous asides not available to the others, and I started to watch the daily dramas with anticipation.

One early example: Ron would occasionally launch into pedantic lectures for the benefit of his benighted crew. A nice gesture, but usually on some topic upon which he had only a rudimentary grasp, but felt compelled to share with others. Shortly after we began our Humpback filming, the sight of a waving pectoral fin inspired Ron to gather the crew about him to explain how whales and dolphins still had vestigial finger bones, carryovers from the distant time when they were land mammals, (a fact well-known to most evolutionarily-enlightened junior high school biology students who had been paying even the slightest attention, but never mind). Everybody had heard it before, but they were taking it stoically, they were feigning consciousness, when Flip's hand came up at the back of the crowd, playing the anxious student.

"That would mean," he said, eyes widening, "that at some point in their evolution…" exaggerated comprehension dawning on his face, Ron nodding, yes,

yes, "they could have been…must have been…" everyone holding their breath now, "…in*credible*…" yes, yes, Ron encouraged, finally an appreciative audience "…*handball players!*" Ron looked confused as the crew collapsed with laughter. This happened time and again, but he was so self-absorbed he never caught on that Flip was putting him on. It sounds mean-spirited, I know, but you had to have been there. The guy was tedious, and everyone needed the break.

Of course that sort of thing made Flip all right in my book; it was the beginning of a long friendship.

The Fin Fanatics

Despite our little dysfunctional film family, we were getting into some interesting situations with the whales and getting some good footage. I was being introduced to a whole new world.

As we spent our days among the Humpbacks, we got caught up in that world and got to know some of the early graduate-student cetacean researchers who had made their way to Maui to study these mysterious singing whales. They were on shoestring budgets, living in communal rental houses and existing on big bags of rice and the odd fish, every spare penny going into sunscreen and boat gas for their little boats.

The most dogged among these was this young grad student named Jim Darling, with whom we shared a whale-research permit that allowed us to film. He would often be floating near us, hour after hour, day after day in the broiling sun in his little open boat, with zinc oxide slathered on his beak, recording whale positions and behaviors and relaying information to a land-based observation platform ashore.

These researchers were so interesting to me, so dedicated, and so full of theories and observations. We were just trying to film the whales as they passed by; these people were looking further under the surface, trying to understand what was driving the behaviors, trying to establish patterns. It was a whole mindset, a lifestyle, and it was fascinating.

We took to inviting these sun-blasted souls aboard our film boat during lulls in the action on the water, offering shade and a cool drink, and receiving in return the latest discourses on whale behavior theory. We soon struck up friendships and developed a real interest in their research.

Evenings would often find us at one of their rented beach houses or another, eagerly discussing the day's new Humpback revelations over beer and barbequed fish, and anxiously looking forward to heading out and doing it all again the next day. Looking back on it now, the crowd comprised a Who's Who of what was to become a roster of the prominent figures in cetacean research today. In addition to Jim Darling, I remember a parade of inspired students who rotated through Lahaina: Greg Silber, Beth Mathews, John Ford, Graham Ellis, Peter Tyack, Jim and Mary Bird manning the shore station, occasional eminences like Roger Payne and Sylvia Earle dropping by, and the odd celebrity coming out for a day or two. I remember spending a memorable afternoon with astronaut Buzz Aldrin sitting on the top deck watching a Humpback mother and calf drifting slowly around the boat. It was an incredibly exciting and heady time, with new revelations and behaviors being documented almost daily. For example, one remarkable day we got the first synchronized-sound film of a singing humpback, which showed no bubbles issuing from the whale, proving that the sound was made internally, not by expelling breath, as most mammals did to make sound. Incredibly exciting, from a research point of view, and it was contagious being around it.

The days rolled by, and most early mornings would find us out in the calm waters between the islands of Maui, Lanai, and Kahoolawe, looking for the suspended blows of the Humpbacks hanging in the distance, everyone tolerating Ron, then launching the underwater camera crew when a group of passing whales looked cooperative, and always trying for the surface breaching shots with the bow camera.

It was an incredible time, a long blur of sun and blue water and the focus on those huge mysterious Humpback whales. But ultimately, this first immersion into this new world had to end. The film charter finally started winding down, they had gotten all of the footage they came for and more, and it was time for them to go back and begin editing (and past time for them to get some time away from each other).

We had one final glorious day at the end of the charter. We invited all of our friends who had been involved in one way or another with the project, including the entire waitress staff from Kimo's Restaurant, for an Easter morning cruise with the whales. One of the great things about the Sport Diver was the big swim platform across the stern that would allow a half-dozen or so people to hang on with mask and snorkels as we cruised around submerged whales, and it turned out that the ideal whale watching cruising speed was also the perfect speed to create the perfect drag for separating swimsuits from snorkeling waitresses...not that it was planned that way, just one of those miraculous coincidences with which we are occasionally blessed. The whole day went that way.

It was unforgettable. Not only were the whales cooperative that morning, lounging and pirouetting under the boat, but later that afternoon we were all invited to attend the First Annual Invitational Maui Downhill Croquet Tournament hosted by John McVie of the band Fleetwood Mac at his place there in Maui...but that is, as you might imagine, another story.

Tarwhals...still stuck after all these years...

That first film charter experience was pivotal and marked the beginning of a lifelong relationship with whales for most of us; some indelible mysterious mark was made on our psyches. After that charter was over, we boat crew went back for the time being to our fishing, but, more and more frequently, other Humpback whale filming opportunities came our way, and we were eager to jump back into the fray.

Whale research expanded, evolved, and became better funded, and our early group kept in contact with each other as the years went by. Many of us would go on to other pursuits, but we always gravitated back to being involved in some aspect of whale research when the opportunity presented itself.

Not only did that first core group of researchers go on to become the leading lights in cetacean research worldwide, but Flip Nicklin went on to photograph most of the whale stories for *National Geographic* magazine over the next few decades, and I was fortunate enough to be involved in some of them.

Today, if you looked down from that same great height, the basic core of Old Lahaina town and its harbor would look remarkably unchanged—if you didn't peer in too closely; a timeless pocket surrounded by sprawling resorts and golf courses. It is a different cast of drug dealers and homeless guys and harbor rats, of course. And a significant number of the tour boats coming and going now hold whale-watchers; whale watching has become an increasingly popular activity, not only in Hawaii, but worldwide. Alongside the whale watching boats, whale research groups from all over the world still come and go from the harbor, with new Humpback whale behaviors and discoveries still being documented regularly; somehow they keep surprising us.

The cannery building that housed the laundry is now a shopping mall, and the Sport Diver and the Black Coral Divers are gone, but Kimo's and the Pioneer Inn are still thriving, and Tad has a shiny new boat in the old slip. And when the sun is going down and the light is just right, some of the characters shuffling around at the far end of the harbor look unsavory enough that if you squint your eyes a bit, it's almost like being back in the old days.

The Great Shark Caper

Just when you thought it was safe...

This was going to be different. We first heard about this upcoming shark adventure from Tad Luckey's wife, Cindy. She came wheeling down to Lahaina Harbor one morning on her bicycle, her faithful companion Auk'we, the Big White Boat Dog, bright red scarf around his neck, galloping alongside the bike as usual. She was obviously excited about something, she was yelling, "A whole week, a whole week...."

We were down on the Sport Diver, me, Tad, and Bear the Deckhand, doing routine maintenance, changing oil, cleaning equipment, replacing lines and the like. The tourist sport fishing season was almost over and business was slowing down, so any possible charter opportunity was a big deal.

Cindy (the business brains of the outfit) had just gotten off the phone with Flip Nicklin, and it seemed he had sold the *National Geographic* magazine on a shark story idea, and he wanted to rent Sport Diver again to try to get some Maui shark pictures.

This was great news. When the tourist season slacked off in Maui, we would turn to bottom fishing and the odd special local charter; the off-season was lean economic times for us, so any business was welcome; besides, this sounded like fun, and we were really looking forward to working with Flip again. We didn't have any idea how to hunt for sharks; to us, they were a nuisance that would chomp our fish catches in half as we were reeling them in, but we had seen enough of them to have an idea where they might be found.

This charter was going to start in a few days and was going to include not only Flip, but also the famous *National Geographic* underwater photographer David Doubilet, whose work I had admired for years. This was indeed the big leagues. Flip was just starting out and hadn't yet made his mark, but David's stuff at the time set the world standard for underwater photography, and I was anxious to meet him.

Offal glad to be aboard

We had to come up with some kind of plan. After all, we couldn't just drive around hoping to run into some sharks; we had to look like we knew what we were doing. We needed shark bait.

So we put a big plastic garbage can on the back deck of Sport Diver and went about filling it up with all manner of gruesome stuff we thought a shark might like. We put in fish carcasses, heads and tails and assorted bits and pieces left over after the charter boats around the harbor filleted their catches. We also threw in a lot of old frozen squid we'd been keeping for bottom fishing bait, some stale bread for filler, and put out the word for whatever smelly remnants our friends who worked at Kimo's restaurant might be able to pick out of the trash.

The can quickly filled up. It was impressive. Imagine a barrel full of haggis gone bad. Nasty stuff. We were almost ready.

We made a few test runs but weren't happy with our bait dissemination technique. We tried cruising slowly along, flinging loads of this horrible stuff out at intervals, but it wasn't working. It didn't make a uniform bait trail, and it went through our supply too quickly.

Bear came up with the ideal solution. In retrospect it had to be Bear's idea, because 1) he was the one who was going to be doing it, and 2) historically he didn't respond well to direct requests that he didn't necessarily agree with or come up with on his own. In fact he had quit just a couple of days ago when we were working on the famously slow-flushing Sport Diver toilet and I'd told him to blow on the end of a plugged hose to clear it. Of course I was just joking, but he had quit and stomped off before I had a chance to explain that. We had quickly worked out that miscommunication, but it was obvious that he was delicate and had to be handled with care.

Anyway, his solution was brilliant. The idea was to ladle a big burlap bag full of the pungent mixture, tie the top closed, and tow it behind the boat, occasionally bringing it up on the swim step to reinvigorate it by beating it soundly with a baseball bat. This produced a very nice long-lasting smelly slick, but after a few beatings, it left Bear, bushy beard and all, covered with flecks of questionable substance, but we didn't feel it necessary to point that out to him at the time. Besides, after all, it was his idea.

Slingwraithes...or Have Spear Gun, Will Travel

We figured we were well covered safety-diver-wise for the inshore smaller reef shark business, but for the deep water man-eater action we figured we might need some help. We needed serious allies, a Coastal

Nostra, protection from the rival prison pod. Maritime Mercenaries. So we turned to the Black Coral Divers.

If anyone could go mano-a-mandible with a big shark, it was one of these guys. They cheated death every day with the crazy dives they were doing. They spent a lot of time in deep water full of sharks and had a crazy go-to-hell fearlessness. They possessed lots of tattoos and weapons galore; knives, hatchets, and bang-sticks—shotgun shell firing devices on the end of sling spears. And they were up for anything. At least I assumed they were. I hadn't exchanged more than a few words with any of them; I tried to stay out of their way. But Tad knew a couple of them, they respected him as a fellow diver, and he put out the word we were looking for some help.

Sure enough, an intense-looking but soft-spoken guy named Bart came by the boat that afternoon. It was odd to see a Black Coral Diver out in broad daylight in our part of the harbor; it was like something from Tolkien. He said he'd be willing to sign on. He told us he had his own gear and could supply a couple of the shotgun shell bang-sticks, and to just let him know when we'd be needing him.

Off-Central Casting

The day arrived, and David and Flip showed up at the dock with an impressive pile of gear. This was apparently David's modus operandi; he was a technical artist and used a lot of hardware, but it paid off in the images he got. He didn't look like the famous underwater photographer I had imagined...more like the Rick Moranis character in the movie *Ghostbusters*, but he seemed like a great guy and his pictures spoke for themselves.

We headed out to do a few test runs over the reef south of town to try out the equipment and our bait-spreading system. Everything worked great. Our smelly slick did attract sharks, lots of little black-tipped reef sharks, and we got some good pictures the first day. So far so good...we were shark hunting.

The initial few days of the shark quest were really quite pleasant. We would drift around above the reefs around Maui and Lanai, keeping the front of the boat upwind of the stern where Bear would be growling and flailing away at intervals on the bait bag. Flip and David would slip into the water when some interesting sharks showed up, mostly the reef sharks and the occasional oceanic white-tip, (who seemed benign enough, despite a bad reputation). Mostly, we were just enjoying the company and the conversation. David had a lot of stories and had brought along a great music collection.

One afternoon we were listening to some lyrical banjo thing he was pitching to some friend of his to use as the opening soundtrack for a movie this friend was making. David would get animated talking about it. It seems this guy was making a movie about the famous Flying Tiger squadron who flew the shark-faced (!) P-40 fighters for the Chinese Air Force at the beginning of World War II, and David envisioned this particular piece of music as the background for the opening scene of the movie as the squadron flew over the snow-capped Chinese mountains in pursuit of Japanese fighters. As he explained it, you could see the whole thing; somehow, it fit the image perfectly. We obviously had some time on our hands. At any rate, we were having a ball, idling around in the sun. But, it soon became apparent that we had exhausted the reef shark possibilities; after all, we were here to get shark pictures, and it was time for bigger fish.

Substandard Behavior

We decided we needed to check out some deeper water possibilities, so we thought a visit to the Submarine was in order. The navy had some years ago sunk a decommissioned World War II submarine, the *USS Bluegill*, off the coast of Maui, and it had become a regular dive destination for us. It was resting in about 150 feet of water, the conning tower coming up to about ninety feet, and it attracted a lot of sea life; we had seen fairly large sharks swimming around out in the blue distance when we had been down there on past dives. Of course we weren't going to be doing any bait chumming there; other people would probably be diving that spot in the near future and likely weren't too keen on seeing any more sharks around than necessary, but we figured it was worth a look.

Getting down to the sub was an adventure in itself. Back in those pre-Global Positioning Satellite days, the way we located most of our favorite dive sites was by lining up landmarks on shore and triangulating our way to the neighborhood, then watching the fathometer for a telltale blip. It worked surprisingly well, actually. For example, in this case I remember the technique for finding the sub was to head southwest out of Lahaina, keeping the smokestack of the sugar mill lined up with a certain peak of the West Maui Mountains until we lined up a certain grove of palm trees with a certain valley, and then we know we were close. Then the fun started.

On a wreck dive like the sub, the worst thing you can do is get your anchor line fouled in the wreck you've come to visit, so we had developed a system. When we knew we were close, we would cut the engine and one of us would jump in the water with the anchor and guide its fall to the bottom. It seems kind of crazy looking back on it, but it seemed routine at the time. Plummeting down with the anchor, as soon as the bubbles cleared after jumping in, the designated anchor-setter would look around and spot the conning tower of the sub somewhere down below.

Keeping clear of any obstructions he would then fly the anchor down to a sandy area off to one side or the other of the hull, land down around 150 ft. deep, set the flukes, and then head back up to a more reasonable depth before the nitrogen narcosis buzz started creeping in. Since a diver is only allowed a few minutes at that depth by the dive tables, it would be somebody else's responsibility to go back down there at the end of the dive with an air-bag to float the thing back up to the surface. The system worked great, the only snag we ever encountered was one time when a line from the air bag got tangled around Tad's leg for a quick upside-down trip up, but even that didn't seem like a big deal at the time, we thought it was hilarious. There's a lot to be said for being young and moronic. I miss it

So anyway, down to the sub we went. It was a great dive spot, eerie, this huge submarine, covered with growth and surrounded by schools of fish, sitting on the white sandy bottom, it really was spectacular, like a movie set. But of course no sharks showed up, they knew we were looking for them. Normally I didn't like seeing big shapes swimming around off in the distance when I was down there, it made me very edgy, the boat seemed a long way off when you were looking up at it from those kinds of depths. But this day we really were hoping for a shark or two, all of us circling around the conning tower, peering off into the blue distance. Nothing. It was clear we needed a different approach. Pulling back into the harbor that afternoon the opportunity presented itself. One of the other sport fishing boats had just brought in a big blue marlin, about a 400 pounder, and they were in the process of cutting it up on the pier. That was standard procedure in those days, nobody had heard of "catch and release"; it was "catch and filet" and sell the good parts. What was left after the meat was carved away was a huge carcass, head and tail still attached, which would normally be dragged out to sea and sunk, but it occurred to us that a big smelly marlin carcass might be just the thing to change our luck big-shark-wise. They happily gave us the reeking thing, and we tied it, hanging by the tail, to the swim step of the Sport Diver. We now had real ammunition. We weren't sure what we were going to do with it yet, but we'd figure out something. Tad left word for Bart that we could probably use his help the next day, it seemed time.

Bait Buoy

The next morning found us motoring out of Lahaina, full of high hopes and dragging the big marlin carcass behind us. Bart, the Black Coral Diver, had been waiting for us at the boat. He proved to be, much to my surprise, not only sane, but also sharp, funny, and good company. He fit right in. He was soon swapping diving yarns with Flip and David, and turned out to be this well-read and educated guy. It was like finding out that the dean of your local college had been moonlighting as an outlaw biker. Like the old warrior-scholar-priests, maybe there were still some around. It was a great lesson for me about prejudice and prejudging people and their lifestyles.

We decided to do our shark-attracting business away from where other people were likely to be, so we headed toward the backside of Lanai, away from normal fishing and diving spots. There was a buoy Bart knew about a fair distance offshore, out past the 100 fathom line, and that sounded like as likely a spot as any to try to find some deep water sharks.

We reached the buoy around mid-morning, and spent the next couple of hours slowly cruising around it, dragging the marlin carcass behind us, Bear all the while flailing away at the bait bag, growling and sending fish bits flying. Bart seemed mildly amused; I don't think he had seen anything like this before...I doubt anyone had. But for all the sound and fury, nothing was happening. Not a solitary shark was to be seen. And the weather was picking up.

We decided we'd better start heading back in. The radio was talking about a Kona storm brewing, and we didn't want to be caught out in that. A Kona storm was when the weather came in from the south, the opposite direction from where the normal trade winds blew. Everything was turned around, the lee shore became the unprotected weather shore and all bets were off, what was normally safe haven wasn't, it threw everyone off-kilter. We dumped the last of our bait as we were leaving, but instead of cutting the marlin carcass loose, we decided to tie it off to the buoy so we could come back and check on it later in the event it attracted something, we thought it couldn't hurt.

Shorebound

The weather report was spot on this time. It was blowing the next morning "like stink", as the local guys liked to say, whatever that meant. Anyway it was obvious we weren't going anywhere, it was 'way too rough outside the harbor to even consider going out there, and we even put extra lines on to Sport Diver at the dock; there were whitecaps inside the harbor itself.

Free time presented itself, which wasn't always a good thing back in those days in Lahaina. We decided we would all meet that evening at Kimo's for dinner, and assess the conditions for the next day.

Somehow a bunch of us ended up over at the Pioneer Inn that morning, nursing a few beers and grousing about the weather, and watching the boats bob up and down in the harbor. A Kona wind put everyone on edge, it just wasn't right. It was the kind of wind that made mothers yell at their kids for no reason at all and made cats lie down with dogs, that kind of thing. That wind may have had something to do with the car incident that happened between Trumbo and me later.

Bruised Cruisers

This is probably as good a time as any to explain the whole car situation on Maui. There was a natural hierarchal progression to the distribution of the scores of cheap Japanese rental cars that were shipped to the island continually, a sort of trickle-down effect. The new cars got rented out first to tourists, but the life of a rental car on Maui was, as they say, nasty, brutish, and short. Between the repeated grinding up the 10,000 ft. north face of Haleakula Crater and the punishing pothole-filled trip back around from Hana (the rental car brochures were very specific about not going around that way, but by the time most beleaguered tourists got to the Seven Sacred Puddles, there was no way they were driving back the way they had come), the cars aged quickly. The first few times they changed hands was probably legitimate, but by the time they got to the likes of us, they were officially rust-covered "Maui Cruisers," and any

101

paperwork had long since disappeared. They were often passed along to friends and new arrivals...everyone had one.

I actually had two. They were identical, except one was an ugly, oxidized Baby Blue with rust spots and holes in the floorboards, and the other an ugly, oxidized Sea-Foam Green with rust spots and holes in the floorboards. Two seemed necessary to keep one running. I was continually in need of a water pump or an alternator or a carburetor, and it was handy to swap parts from one to the other.

I say they were identical, but there was one important difference. The blue one, in addition to the normal complement of cockroaches, had a huge cane spider living in it. Cane spiders were supposed to be harmless, but they were terrifying. They normally lived in the sugar cane fields and were overall about the size of a small plate, the hairy middle body about golf-ball-sized, but they were so fast you could never get a good look at one, much less kill it. This particular one had taken up residence in my car and would never show itself unless I was at least slightly hung over and had forgotten completely about it. Then it would suddenly launch itself into frenzied laps, scuttling across the overhead and the sun visor and around under the seat, its legs a whirling blur, me screaming and swatting away, always just missing it; it took a lot out of a guy.

It must have been disconcerting to fellow drivers to see the driver of the car ahead suddenly throw his coffee cup up in the air and start flailing his arms about, the car swerving all over the road, muted screaming coming across the pavement. People make such a big deal these days about texting and talking on a mobile phone being such a driving distraction, that's not even close. Having a giant spider suddenly bombing around inside your car at about a million miles an hour, now *that's* a driving distraction, trust me. It never happened when anyone else was driving with me; I don't think anyone else believed it was there.

The cockroaches weren't shy about showing themselves, however. I remember one night after a particularly grueling dinner at Nimble's Restaurant, Jim Darling had gone down to have a nap in the back seat of that car while Flip and I settled up the bill. When we finally got down to the parking lot, Jim and the take-away dessert carton he was carrying were alive with roaches, hundreds of them; it looked like a scene from a horror movie. We knocked the carton away with a stick and dragged Jim out; he had been sound asleep. I think if we had gotten down there a minute later they would have eaten him. I don't know where they all hid during the day; I think they might have been holding the car together.

Deconstruction Derby

At any rate, I remember it was the blue car I was driving the morning in question when Trumbo claimed I backed into him as I was pulling out of the Pioneer Inn. We had both left the bar at he same time, and he was parked behind me in his own similar cruiser. Trumbo worked on the boat next to ours in the harbor and was a good friend of mine, but he was a little nuts. He reminded me of the actor Martin Mull, only on catnip.

If I did touch his car, it was only a little tap as I was backing up, and it certainly didn't warrant his reaction. Again, it could have been the effect of that Kona wind.

As I pulled out into the lot between the Pioneer Inn and the lighthouse, I heard a noise and turned just in time to see Trumbo in full acceleration mode and heading right for me. I pulled ahead just in time to avoid being broadsided, but he caught me in the stern quarter and spun the car ninety degrees to the right, broken headlights and grill parts flying. I could see Trumbo's face behind his windshield and the steam coming from his broken radiator, looking crazed and laughing maniacally. He was backing up to get another run. Terrified, I managed to get it in reverse and back away far enough that he just clipped my front end, but some vital damage had been done; the front of my car was wobbling violently now, and I could hear the fan clattering against something. He seemed to have stalled. I had to act quickly. I had an opening and was able to back around in a tight circle and get in a satisfying collision backing directly into the side of his door, moving his car a couple of feet to the right, but at some cost to the back of my own car, pieces of taillight and rear bumper scattering across the asphalt.

All the people at the Pioneer Inn bar were on their feet now, some standing on chairs to see what the hell was going on. Who knows what this insanity could have escalated into, but now we could hear sirens off in the distance and figured it was time to leave.

We got the cars pointed toward the alley that ran between the Pioneer Inn and the park, and, spewing steam and fluids and pieces, made our escape. We split up and I somehow made it all the way back to my place, wobbling and clattering. Trumbo apparently wasn't so lucky. I heard later he'd had to abandon his vehicle and flee on foot when it overheated and seized up, but it served him right; he was the one who'd started it.

I had made it back home, but I was down to one car now, the blue one never moved under its own power again. I'm sure the cockroaches made out all right, but I often wondered what happened to the cane spider now that it didn't have any real job; I hoped it would be okay.

The day was still young, but I was already worn out and we still had the evening festivities ahead. This time off business was exhausting; we needed to get back to work.

Other Sirens in the Night

Dinner at Kimo's was at the least a regular weekly tradition. We had gotten to know everyone there well during the previous year's whale movie making days and had taken the staff out on the boat on several occasions since then. In fact, Tracy, one of the waitresses, was now my regular girlfriend, so dinner there was always a lively affair, and we had made the place a kind of unofficial headquarters.

Everyone showed up on time, hungry as usual. Tracy had the night off so was joining us, and we were shown to our favorite table, the big one upstairs overlooking the bar and the ocean. My friend Wayne-Dog, of impeccable handlebar moustache fame, was bartending, which was always a good sign. Wayne-Dog and Trumbo and I had recently gotten in a bit over our heads when we had somehow gotten entered into the Wild Cow Milking Contest at the last Maui Upcountry Rodeo a few weeks before, and we were still recovering from that, but that's another story.

Dinner was fantastic; the fresh fish and ribs in plum sauce the restaurant was famous for showed up in fine form, drinks and laughter were all flowing, life was good. And the weather looked like it was easing; it looked like we'd be able to get back out on the water the next day.

Dinner was winding down when a bunch of the waitresses came by the table and announced that there was a new club opening at the resort up the road. They were going there to check it out for a bit, and maybe do a little dancing, and wondered if any of us wanted to join them. David had an endearing quality to him, and they had been flirting shamelessly with him all night. He didn't have a chance.

Now it must be said that the waitress staff at Kimo's could initially have an unusual effect on some people when meeting them for the first time. For one thing, they looked collectively like some beauty pageant had been unnecessarily given an extreme makeover. Their slinky outfits were made of giant flower prints, and that visual stimulation coupled with the fresh flowers in their hair made some deep part of the male insect brain, consciously or unconsciously, think pollination, the hypothalamus quacking like a duck. But this was only outwardly manifested by a slight glazing of the eyes and a stammer. Before anyone else could say or do anything, David stammered that he would be delighted, and before we, (or probably he), knew it, they were gone, just a lingering floral scent in the air and an empty seat where David had just been sitting. No one else had time to respond.

Dessert came and went, and then after-dinner cordials, and then the restaurant was shutting down, the big iron-barred doors facing Front Street closing. And still no David. We were just beginning to get worried; it was time to go home and get a little sleep for the next day, when he finally showed up. He was hanging on to the bars of the front gate, disheveled and out of breath, his glasses crooked and hair sticking out at all angles. We

106

asked him what had happened, where he'd been. He was trying to say something:

"Trapped..." he croaked, "...Beneath the Planet of the Ultra-Disco-Vixens." That was all he said. Even the Kimo's girls seemed coy when we asked them about it later, although it was probably just a routine evening for them; the whole night remains a mystery.

Peril

The ocean was still rough the next morning from the passing storm but definitely navigable. It was the last day of the charter period, and we were all anxious to get back out to our buoy to see if our marlin had indeed attracted anything interesting. Everybody was in fine form on the trip out, no apparent ill effects from the previous night; in fact, there was no mention of the night at all; it was as if it had never happened.

I remember we were passing around books we were reading (a lot of time underway on long boat trips is spent by reading one thing or another), and I remember Bart's contribution was a book I read later called *Turtle Diaries*, about a couple of conservation-minded Londoners who freed captive turtles from the London Zoo. About as unlikely a choice of reading material as I could have imagined only days ago for a Black Coral Diver, I would have bet any amount of money against it, but I was still learning how narrow-minded my prejudices had been.

When we arrived at our buoy, it was obvious something was happening. Lots of birds were circling around, and we could see schools of little fish darting around under the surface. The surface was still a little rough; we needed to get under there to see what was going on.

We slowly circled the area as we gathered all the gear together, and just Flip, David, and Bart suited up. We didn't need any extra personnel in the water here cluttering up the shoot, which was fine with me. It seemed spooky out there.

And it turned out it was spooky indeed. I never did get a totally clear picture of what went on underneath the water that morning. I backed Sport Diver over near the buoy and killed the engine, and the divers headed down. It was some minutes later that we heard the shot, very loud and very clear, vibrating through the hull. It scared the hell out of us on the boat. The guys showed up shortly thereafter, scrambling onto the swim step, clearly shaken. It was some time before some sort of coherent story emerged.

This is what I was able to piece together later: It seemed there had been a lot of activity around the buoy. Remnants of the marlin carcass were still there, not much, but enough so that a food chain of sorts was still in attendance, lots of little fish darting in and out, with bigger predators circling and feeding on them. And down deep were even bigger predators, big sharks circling slowly. Flip told me later he thought they were something called Dusky Sharks. I'd never heard of them.

It all looked like a perfect setup for some great pictures, until the big sharks started a disturbing behavior; they began repeatedly rocketing up from the depths straight at the divers, veering off at the last second. Each pass was a little closer; the biggest of the sharks was acting aggressive, bunching its body up on the latest pass. It seemed one of our party managed to get behind the rudder of the boat, but there really wasn't any place to hide and not enough time between passes to try to make it back in the boat.

108

The last pass had been too close, this was not going well, and Bart made a decision. He took the safety clip out of the bang stick. This would allow the force of the impact of the spear to force the shotgun shell back against the firing pin of the chamber and detonate it out the end as it impacted. It wasn't anything you wanted to do unless you had to, but this was looking like one of those times.

The next time the big shark swooped up, headed right for them, Bart unleashed the sling and caught the shark between the eyes, the concussion of the explosion killing it instantly, its momentum carrying it past the divers and down back into the deep. Again, not what any of us wanted...we just wanted pictures; no one had anticipated this instant aggression from the sharks.

I guess I was feeling some remorse as well as relief as we started back towards home. Of course there was no question the shark had to be killed when it was clearly threatening us (besides, the last payment for the charter hadn't been paid yet. How would we explain it to Cindy if the clients had gotten eaten?). The question was whether we had crossed a line by attracting the animals there in the first place, even if we didn't anticipate the outcome. I know Flip was thinking the same thing. We talked about it later. I'm not sure what Bart was thinking; he was quietly reading about saving turtles.

As for David, he had twice escaped from a perilous situation in as many days; first the Ultra Disco Vixens incident and now this — and he wasn't showing any inclination to talk about either of them, not now and not likely ever. It was a somber boat ride back to Lahaina, everyone seemingly in a reflective mood. One thing was certain: the Maui portion of the shark story had ended. We weren't going to be pulling off a stunt like this again any time soon.

Hai Noon in Lahaina

Back in the Saddle Again

After the hoopla following the release of the first IMAX whale film featuring the Maui Humpbacks, Lahaina was the focus of film groups from all over, and Cindy got word that a Japanese film crew wanted to charter Tad Luckey's boat Sport Diver for a couple of weeks. Fantastic news, it looked like we were back in the whale business.

It turned out Flip Nicklin and several research groups had recommended us; there weren't too many operators who had any experience working around the whales back then, so I guess the fact that we had done it at all made us de facto experts. At any rate, this was great news, and we were anxious to get back out there.

This was of course our first experience working with a foreign film crew, we didn't have any idea what to expect. We didn't know it at the time, but this was the beginning of a long-lasting relationship with the Japanese film community. Flip and all of us ended up becoming good friends and doing years of work with a guy named Koji Nakamura, already a famous photographer in Japan, but, on this first adventure, we weren't sure how to prepare. For my part, I started re-reading James Clavell's novel *Shogun* as my homework assignment. I remembered that it contained a lot of useful Japanese vocabulary and info, full of terms like *hai, dozo, domo* (yes, please, thank you); it actually turned out to be quite helpful.

We found out around this time that one of our team, namely Bear the Deckhand, was in fact a resident of Canada and would be required by U.S. Immigration to go back there for a time (like right away), so we suddenly found ourselves in need of a replacement deckhand.

We had run into a guy named Cowboy (that is how he actually introduced himself) some time earlier. He was a character who hung out around the harbor looking to get on with a fishing boat, and he seemed he might be a likely candidate. And he really was a cowboy, a tall, rangy, mournful-looking son of Kansas, complete with a propensity for cowboy boots and a cheek full of chewing tobacco. He wasn't wearing a cowboy hat here, but he did wear a varied collection of John Deere and DeKalb Seed baseball caps that could only have come with him from his native state. I got the impression he hadn't been in Maui all that long.

We knew he was an actual cowboy after we had seen him ride a bull at the Maui Upcountry Rodeo, a real honest-to-God Hawaiian Paniolo rodeo. This was the same day that Trumbo, Wayne-Dog, and I had ill-advisedly gotten ourselves entered into the Wild Cow Milking Contest, another clear indication that none of us had much sense back then.

This contest was the spectacle in which an unfortunate lactating cow was set upon by a team of three bovine molesters racing against other teams, two people on horseback and one on foot. The idea was that the team that could first immobilize the frenzied cow and then get a recognizable quantity of milk from it into a beer bottle, and then deliver it across the finish line in the shortest amount of time would win. The ASPCA seemed to be noticeably absent at these events.

And we had no business being there, but we had talked some people into loaning us horses and gear on the spot (a couple of us actually had some small horseback experience, and somehow apparently had pitched a good line). But what we were really enjoying was reeling around the place playing cowpokes with official numbers on our backs, until the time came when we were actually called upon to perform and there was no sign of Wayne-Dog. We were hunting high and low. The event was imminent; the announcer was announcing us, and still no Dog. We spotted a crowd down around the horse trailers. It seemed a horse had trapped someone against a fence; the horse was rubbing itself along it, and you could see someone's legs flailing beneath the horse's belly. The horse was clearly enjoying itself, but somebody was getting roughed up.

Of course it was Wayne-Dog. The crowd managed to get the horse disengaged from the fence, and there was the disheveled Dog. "He likes me," he announced with a goofy grin showing beneath his tousled handlebar moustache, and then we knew he was in no condition to even get aboard the animal, much less perform in public. The whole thing was embarrassing and best forgotten about as soon as possible.

Later, we saw Cowboy had entered himself in the Bull Riding event and actually acquitted himself well, which was no small feat; there were a lot of real cowboys on Maui. You had to be crazy to get on one of those bulls; it was dangerous as hell, and we were impressed.

So Cowboy came aboard as replacement deckhand. He wasn't a fast and motivated worker, but he was fun and full of stories, so he fit right in.

We had a few days before the film crew arrived, so we had a chance to run a few fishing trips with Cowboy to get him tuned up in the deckhand department. I remember one of the first charters I worked with him on, it turned out to be one of the most bizarre trips we ever had. It came about like this:

Eastern meets The Western

A mysterious group showed up at the harbor one morning, it was obviously some type of cult. A large woman dressed in a white robe was being attended to by a number of similarly clad sycophants, some hovering around her while an advance group cleared the way ahead.

The handler or facilitator or whatever he was approached us on the dock and inquired about taking a boat ride, so we sold them a half day fishing charter, and the deal was arranged. There were some ground rules he needed to tell us about, however, chief among them being that we were not to address the large woman in white directly, that any communication that took place must be through one of the intermediaries, preferably himself. That wasn't going to be a problem for us; in fact the less communication we had with this group the better we were going to like it, it all seemed very weird.

They all came aboard and arranged themselves around the big woman, and we started off. So far so good. Cowboy got the fishing poles and lines out in good shape, assigned everyone a pole, and we started fishing along the reefs south of town, a beautiful and serene day to be out on the water.

This group was clearly bothering Cowboy, though, he kept giving them odd looks, trying to figure them out. Then they began this chanting business, a rhythmic kind of singing, which wasn't helping; you could see it was getting on his nerves. At one point I heard him growl at one of the group, "Why don't you sing somethin' we all know?" I was about to intervene, when a fish hit one of the outrigger lines with a loud snap, and the reel exploded into a deafening whine as the line went screaming off. It was something big.

Cowboy got everything cleared out of the way and got the guy whose pole it was, a pale skinny kid, strapped down in the fighting chair and was screaming "Reel! Reel!" into his ear. The kid looked scared; he was churning the handle for all he was worth. Everybody else was bunched up in a panicked knot at the other end of the cockpit.

The fish came up to leader behind the boat, and it was a nice one, about a thirty pound *ono*. The thing about the *ono*, (which we had been drilling into Cowboy), was that you wanted to dispatch them quickly because they were very aggressive and had these incredibly sharp teeth, like a barracuda, and could be dangerous when they came aboard. Usually one good whack with the baseball bat right on top of the head as they slid onto the swim step would do it, but it had to be precise and took a little practice.

This first time didn't go well. He only managed to give the fish a glancing blow as he pulled it aboard, just enough to enrage it, as it went sliding into the boat toward the huddled group, jaws snapping horribly. Cowboy then panicked and went after the thing with the baseball bat like he was killing rattlesnakes back home on the ranch, flailing away, blood and brains and eyeballs flying everywhere. He was pretty worked up; the fish was becoming unrecognizable. But he did finally manage to subdue it, although at some messy cost to the inside of the boat, the walls, the overhead, the white robes. Everything. The whole place was covered with blood and goo, including the clients. It looked like the scene of a massacre.

The effect on the group you can only imagine. The big woman's mouth was working, but no sound was coming out. I think they were actually in physical shock; they didn't look so good. I'm not sure what they expected when they signed up for a fishing charter, but it certainly wasn't this. The facilitator guy wasn't actually able to get any words out either, but he made it clear that they wanted to go back in, like right now; they didn't want to fish anymore. The minute we hit the dock, they all scrambled away, listing in various directions, some leaning against each other. There wasn't even a mention of a tip, which disgusted Cowboy.

It was obvious there were some rough edges to be smoothed out. We'd have to work on Cowboy's technique later. But for now, we had a whale film crew showing up the next day and had some cleaning up to do.

Just Nippon Over Anytime

The film group arrived right on schedule, and you could tell from that first day that this was going to be interesting. There were six of them: Ishi, the older guy who was obviously in charge, and four younger guys, and a beautiful young woman, Akiko. Cindy had been in communication with Ishi to set up their arrangements, the food they wanted onboard, etc. Luckily Lahaina had a number of excellent Japanese delis, so ordering a daily delivery of Bento lunches, the traditional box lunch of rice, fish, pickled vegetables, and teriyaki was no problem. In addition, they had asked specifically for Sara Lee, which seemed a little odd. Cindy asked what kind. "Just regular kind" was the response, so she started with a large carrot cake.

They piled an amazing quantity of gear aboard, lots of cameras and housings in addition to all their dive gear. We decided that all three of us, Tad, Cowboy, and I, should all go along on these trips, not only were we anxious to make a good impression, but there was going to be a lot going on with six divers and all their cameras.

We finally set out of the harbor late that morning headed for the channel between Maui and Lanai, as likely a spot as any to encounter some Humpbacks, while the group went about organizing their stuff, putting on their dive gear and adjusting things. We started to get to know one another.

It turned out Ishi was the only one who spoke any real English, but not much. Akiko had just a smattering and the others none at all. But they were friendly and enthusiastic and in general seemed delightful.

We hadn't been out too long, the group in the back of the boat for the moment and us looking out front scanning the horizon for whale blows. Tad spotted a blow, quite a distance away toward Lanai, and thinking the group would like to see their first indication of humpbacks, called out, "Ishi...Whale!" and pointed toward Lanai. Ishi's eyes got big. "Ahhh!" he said.

We motored on for a time, hoping to see the blow again, but then Cowboy went back to check on the group and came back with some news.

"I hate to tell you this, boss, but it looks like it's just us." He had a way with a pithy phrase.

Sure enough, they were gone.

"Holy Mackerel!" Tad said, or something to that effect, and he spun the boat around and we could just make out in the far distance heads bobbing around in the water in the channel behind us.

This wouldn't do. We went back and gathered everyone back up aboard and explained to them the absolute necessity of communicating with us and each other before any diving took place, that when someone said "whale" it didn't necessarily mean a call to jump in, all the while Ishi translating this, with the attentive row of heads bobbing earnestly, a sight we would come to know well. We figured we'd had enough excitement for the first day; everybody seemed a bit worn out. I know I was. I'd never lost anyone overboard, much less the whole charter. We took a leisurely cruise back to Lahaina, taking in the sights, figuring to get a fresh start the next morning.

After we got back to the dock, we thought we would celebrate our survival by passing out a round of beers (our normal habit at the time), and this was where Cowboy really established his stature in the eyes of our guests. Apparently twist-off bottle caps were unheard of in Japan, so when he casually began twisting caps off bottles and passing them around, it occasioned a great deal of wide-eyed talk and admiration—apparently, to them, it was akin to seeing someone change a tire without a lug nut wrench. From that moment on, any time a bottle needed opening it was taken to the big *gaigin* with the hands of steel, to be quickly and humbly opened with a flourish, and that always prompted reverential exclamations of amazement. He apparently never did feel the need to explain the twist-off cap phenomenon.

Haierarchy

The next day we settled into our routine, and it was working out well. We would head out into the channels between Maui, Lanai, and Molokai, easing up on surface active groups of humpbacks, and finding the occasional mother and calf pair, the group taking to the water when conditions looked good, and we were getting into some good filming situations.

It was fascinating to see how the group dynamics worked on a Japanese film crew. Everyone dove, of course, but the two youngest guys did almost all of the real work, all of the hauling, cleaning, packing, picking up, everything. The other two guys busied themselves with some administrative chores and bossed the young guys around, but didn't involve themselves in any real labor, and the head guy, Ishi, didn't seem to have any chores at all. It looked like a great system, the expectation being that the young guy would get to be the middle guy over time, then the head guy eventually. It was a perfect example of goal postponement, toil today with an eventual future of ease, like becoming the queen ant in the colony (only, in the ant colony, the queen's legs eventually fall off from lack of use after she swells up to gargantuan size, but never mind). Anyway, it seemed to work and everybody seemed happy about it.

Akiko didn't fit into this hierarchy; she was outside and above it. Not only was she the beautiful model for the film shoot, it turned out she was also the daughter of the producer (or someone important, I was never clear who), and she was definitely treated with proper royal deference. And she was extraordinary, always smiling and beautiful and graceful, a delightful princess. We were all a little smitten.

But none so much as Cowboy. He fell immediately and totally in love. From the first day, he took to mooning around after her with a goofy expression on his mournful face, fussing over her dive gear and generally getting in the way. Everyone, including Akiko, pretended not to notice, but it was pretty clear the state he was in, poor guy. It just didn't seem likely to work out. I'm not sure what, if anything, he was thinking. (Visions of him and his gal pushing Kobe Beef along the Aikido Trail?) I was just hoping he'd eventually get over it and that it wasn't as glaringly obvious to everyone else as it was to me, but everybody seemed to be dutifully ignoring the whole thing.

Partners Without Parrots

Things were otherwise going along swimmingly, despite the language difficulties. It was strange, though, they kept asking for Sara Lee, although they didn't seem to be eating much of it, so the stuff was piling up. They had hardly touched the carrot cake, so Cindy tried various other varieties: Cinnamon Swirl, Strawberries and Cream, even some cheesecakes, but nothing seemed to be hitting the mark. Again, when asked what kind of Sara Lee they would prefer, Ishi would respond "regular kind," so it was a mystery. We figured we would eventually find the right variety if we kept bringing a different kind every day.

A few days later, Ishi invited us all to dinner to celebrate how well the filming was going, but, unfortunately, I had another engagement and couldn't make it that particular night, and it turned out at the last minute that one of Tad and Cindy's beloved pet parrots had died, so they begged off as well, but Cowboy was available.

It apparently all started off great, in hearing about it later. They had arranged for the usual big table at Kimo's, and everybody was in a festive mood; Cowboy was in his element, seated next to Akiko with no competition. The group quickly ran into some communication problems, however, when Cowboy relayed Tad's regrets about missing the gathering because of the death of one of his parrots. Of course this sobered the group quickly, misunderstanding that one of Tad's parents had died. As Ishi translated, the group grew quiet and wide-eyed, lots of "Ahhhhs" and distraught head nodding, which shook Cowboy; he hadn't realized that Japanese would be so fond of parrots. The party was definitely taking a solemn turn.

When Ishi asked if they should cancel tomorrow's trip, given this sad news, and if they would possibly be seeing Tad tomorrow, Cowboy responded brightly, desperately trying to turn the mood around, "Heck yeah. It's no big deal. Besides, that parrot had liked Cindy a lot better than Tad anyway. Sucker would try to bite him on the ear every time he turned his back." The ensuing mistranslation brought another round of "Ahhhhs" and even wider eyes, and no small amount of confusion; it seemed disrespectful not to honor a dead parent after all. It eventually all got sorted out, but the mood was broken; it seemed the dinner party never really recovered after that.

Honor Bound and Down

We were getting better and better filming opportunities as the days went by; we were discovering that sometimes it was better to wait quietly for situations to develop instead of motoring madly from place to place hoping to find some great behavior.

120

One afternoon after lunch, we were sleepily drifting along in close to shore where we had seen a blow earlier when Tad mentioned to Ishi that perhaps they would like to dive on the whale right under them, and pointed down to a large humpback suspended motionless under the boat. Pandemonium ensued as gear was thrown on and the group took to the water. One of the young guys apparently was a little hasty in assembling his camera housing, because it immediately filled with water when he got in, and the resulting negative buoyancy began taking him deeper. The deeper he went, the less lift he had, and the combined weight of the flooded camera and housing were soon too much for his buoyancy compensator vest to overcome, and he was being dragged to the bottom. But he refused to let go.

Luckily it was only a little over a hundred feet deep where we were, so he ended up landing on the bottom in a cloud of silt with his camera, and we were able to head down with a float bag to retrieve it and him. If it had been deeper, I wonder if he would ever have let go of that camera; it was his responsibility, and he was embarrassed later by the whole affair. It may be a cultural difference, but I don't think I know many people who would ever consider risking their life for a flooded camera.

The Cowboy Suit

Cowboy had a problem. The charter was winding down and he hadn't made a connection with his Akiko. Desperate measures were called for. He decided to ask her on a dinner date. He screwed up his courage and went about it formally, approaching Ishi first with his request. Ishi responded that dinner would be fine, very nice. Akiko seemed amenable as well; it was arranged for the following night. The stars were out in Cowboy heaven…he was riding on air.

The appointed night came, boots were polished, finery was donned, whiskers were trimmed, and off he went, a confident man.

It wasn't much later that the call came. There had been some misunderstanding, not just Akiko but the whole group was waiting there at the restaurant, ready to eat, and some financial assistance was going to be required, could Tad come down with a credit card? He was crushed. I'm not sure how the rest of the big dinner went; he seemed reluctant to talk about it later.

Sara Lee Stalks

The charter was coming to an end, and except for certain rebuffed romantic overtures, it had gone exceedingly well. Cowboy seemed resigned, resilient Westerner, he would recover. The group had gotten more than they had hoped for film-wise, and the experience, despite the language challenges, had been delightful. This was, as I mentioned, the start of a long relationship with the Japanese film community.

As we were leaving the dock on that last morning, a final piece of the puzzle fell into place. Ishi was chewing on a piece of celery from a big bag of celery stalks he had recently taken to bringing to the boat every morning and carrying around. He offered Cowboy one. "Sara Lee?" he asked.

"Sure, don't mind if I do," Cowboy said, light bulbs going off. "Ahhh…" he said.

Castaways on Coconut Island –
Sharks, Pigs and Darwin's Crabs

Everybody's Fantasy Island

Flip was off on a new tack. His latest story proposal to *National Geographic* magazine didn't have anything to do with the usual suspects, the whales and dolphins he normally specialized in (although it did involve some sharks, a sometime subject of his). He was interested in an island, *Isla de Cocos*, a legendary island we'd all heard about for years.

His pitch to the magazine was that there was so much going on at this lonely spot of land, Cocos Island, 300 miles off the Pacific Coast of Central America, that the island itself could serve as the subject of a story, and they agreed.

There was a lot to be said for the idea. We had heard so many stories about this island that it had taken on an almost mythical status for us. It was by all accounts an incredible place. For starters it was totally isolated, reportedly the largest uninhabited island in the world, emerging all by itself in a vast expanse of ocean, even crowning its own small tectonic plate, the Cocos Plate. The diversity and quantity of sea life attracted to such a place would have to be incredible. Indeed the reports from people who had scuba dived there were so outrageous as to scarcely be believed; stories of huge schools of hammerhead sharks, giant whale sharks, and copious sea life. And its isolation was such that, like the Galapagos, many of its animal and plant species were endemic, found nowhere else.

I began studying up on it when Flip first started talking about doing a story there, and it seemed the legends and lore surrounding the island were legion. It was said to have been a favorite haunt of pirates through the centuries, and reports of buried treasure allegedly cached there were so pervasive that in the intervening years hundreds of expeditions had been launched to the island to search for one reported vast treasure or another (even one reported attempt by Franklin Delano Roosevelt while on a fishing trip in the area). One estimate put the accumulated treasure, if it was indeed all still there, at over a billion dollars. But if any of the legendary treasures had ever been found, no one was talking about it.

If all that weren't enough, Cocos was also reportedly the model island author Daniel Defoe used as the backdrop for his book *Robinson Crusoe*, and more recently the setting used by Michael Crichton for his book *Jurassic Park* (although he called it *Isla Nublar*, or Cloudy Island, an apt name, given that its higher elevations are in continual cloud cover).

Anyway, it sounded like an interesting place, and when Flip said he'd probably need an assistant, I immediately lobbied for the position and cleared my schedule; I had to see this. I had visions of white sandy beaches, gentle surf, coconut palms, and (unbidden, not my fault) even a blue lagoon with maybe Brooke Shields in it.

Flip figured the best way to get out there was on a live-aboard commercial dive boat that was beginning to make regular trips with recreational divers out to the island from Costa Rica. The boat was called the *Okeanos*, one of the Aggressor Diving Fleet that specialized in doing high-end diving adventures to exotic destinations all over the world. The plan was to get in some diving around the island coming and going with them and to talk them into letting us off on the island in between their trips. A good plan as far as it went; all we needed now was permission. Costa Rica, whose territory the island was, apparently frowned on people going ashore there. In years past, they had maintained a couple of soldiers as a naval attachment there to discourage visitors and treasure hunters.

You had to wonder what kind of trouble those poor navy swabs had gotten themselves into to merit that assignment. And to wonder about their mental health. I had heard stories from people I knew and trusted about wild-eyed soldiers there inviting visiting yachtsmen to go on feral pig hunts with them using their automatic weapons, and the visitors being too frightened to refuse. Nice. Now there's an excursion you don't read about much in the travel brochures. But, around this time, the country was in the process of declaring the island a national park, so apparently the soldiers were being replaced by park rangers, which seemed to bode well for our mission and us.

Getting the green light for the assignment, Flip loosed the staff that did those sorts of things at the magazine on the project, and they came through, as they normally did, with flying colors. The National Geographic name carried a lot of weight. It turned out Costa Rica would give us special permission to camp on the island, and the dive boat would transport us out there and back.

We started making plans to pull this off. We decided it would be best to stage this adventure mostly from Costa Rica, taking down with us only the necessary photographic equipment and minimal diving and camping stuff, and getting the rest of what we needed down there.

I contacted an old college friend (and former Kimo's waitress from Lahaina), Mary Miller, for some help. She had moved down there some years ago with her crazy Texan friend, Rob, whom she'd met on one of her sailing adventures. They had settled in. The last time I'd seen them was a couple of years before when they had been caretaking a vast macadamia nut plantation on the east side of the country and I had paid them a memorable visit.

After-Glowworms

I was working at the time in Panama, just across the border from Costa Rica, running a ship for Exploration Cruise Lines, and I wanted to sneak away for awhile on my break with my lovely then-girlfriend Cherie (now my lovely wife), who also worked aboard the ship as a chef. Since the company management forbade onboard liaisons, we thought we'd get out of the country on our mutual time off, and a visit with Rob and Mary seemed like just the ticket.

We knew it was time to get away because we'd just had a close call a few nights before when I had gone down to the crew quarters to see if she was still awake, and as I bent down to peer under her door to see if her light was on, a deckhand suddenly rounded the corner, and I was caught like a deer in the headlights. It was a near thing.

"Captain?" he said, a quizzical look on his face. "All of these baseboards need to be sanded down to bare metal, re-primered, and painted," I told him. I didn't have time to think, it just came out. "Yes, sir," he said (being one of the polite ones). It had been a close call. The deckhands needed a project anyway, and the baseboards did need a new coat of paint, but that kind of thing took a lot out of me, so, as I mentioned, we were looking forward to getting off the boat and out of the territory for awhile.

Anyway, Rob and Mary were expecting us; they had lots of room, they told us, and there was a big plantation house we could stay in. The grounds were huge; they kept a stable of horses for getting around. It all sounded fantastic, and it turned out to be even better than advertised.

We took a short flight to the city of Limon, hopped a bus, and were soon in a magical place. On the big front porch of an old plantation home, we were visiting with our old friends with cool drinks in hand, surrounded by huge trees and a setting sun. As darkness fell, we could see that the trees were covered by hundreds of glowworms and fireflies. What a sight. We went out and walked among these trees, everything sparkling and blinking...Cherie caught a firefly in a jar to keep as a reminder of that night, and it lived for weeks in her room back on the ship.

The next morning we saddled up the horses for a tour of the place, galloping along through manicured lines of macadamia trees, the sun shining through the leaves. The experience was romantic and dreamlike, and the memory remains that way for both Cherie and me to this day.

127

I hadn't seen Rob and Mary since then and was looking forward to reconnecting with them.

T for Tico, T for Texas

They had moved on, Mary told me excitedly on the phone when I called to tell them about our upcoming adventure, they were now in the process of starting their own nature lodge on the Pacific side of Costa Rica near Drake Bay. Fortunately for us, they were both going to be in the capital city, San Jose, getting supplies around the time we were going to be heading down there, and would be happy to meet up and help get us set up for our project. Good news: local knowledge was invaluable when starting out on a deal like this.

I gathered up my usual gear (except, sadly, for my solar-powered pith helmet, which had dissolved where I had left it under a tarp in the garage). Flip decided that since we were going to be going aboard a fancy dive boat with real divers, and since neither of us had done any recreational diving for awhile and we didn't want to embarrass ourselves, we'd better trade up to some of the fancy newer equipment: better masks and snorkels, new lighter wetsuits, and most importantly, something unfamiliar to either of us (but which seemed like a very good idea), one of the new automatic dive computers. We had always used the old dive tables, manually figuring and logging times, but these new gizmos went along with the diver and calculated bottom times and decompression stops, and even took into account the times between dives—pretty neat. Flip picked one up; we figured we would learn how to use it when we got down there.

We flew in to San Jose, and I was again struck by what a beautiful place this capital of Costa Rica was, nestled high in its cradle of volcanoes. It is called the

"City of Perpetual Springtime" with good reason, because at its elevation of around 5,000 ft. the weather is usually balmy, and flowers grow everywhere year-round. It's an inviting place.

Rob and Mary had offered to meet us at the airport to take us to our hotel, and as we waited at the curb I guess I should have been prepared for the rig that came wheeling up to get us, Rob after all being a native son of Texas, but it still took me a little by surprise, along with the rest of the crowd at the airport. Rob had souped up his old VW microbus, putting in a powerful engine and mounting huge steer horns on the front, along with the largest truck air horn arrangement he could find. It was painted bright yellow and made quite an impression.

Amid flurries of honking (the thing actually played different tunes), greetings and hugs from Mary, we piled in and headed for the hotel, getting a little background on the new vehicle en route. As Rob explained it, they had been making regular delivery trips to their new lodge on the treacherous highway between San Jose and the Pacific coast, a grueling stress test of a trip, a steep and winding high-speed traffic hell. One day they had simply had enough of being intimidated by the situation, and had decided to fight back. No more getting blown off the road in their underpowered van by the barreling big lumber rigs and crazed produce trucks careening around the road. He had set out to equal the playing field, and this masterpiece was the result. You could tell he was more than a little proud of it, Mary, too.

They hadn't had a chance to try it out yet, but they would be heading back down to their lodge in a few days and asked us if we wanted to ride along. The timing was perfect. They could give us a ride to our appointment with the dive boat in Puntarenas. I couldn't wait.

In the meantime, Mary got us all lined out with the various hardware and camping stores we needed to visit in San Jose, and we started amassing our gear, sleeping bags and mats, a small stove and cooking utensils, and lots of little detail items like can openers and flashlights. We stocked up on some of the dry stores like pasta and cereals we thought we'd need, planning to get fresh produce in Puntarenas just before leaving. We were getting quite a cache in the hotel rooms between the gear we'd brought and the boxes of this new stuff.

Rey del Camino

The planned departure day arrived, and we were able to squeeze all of our supplies, gear, and food into the new machine and head out. We looked like the Joad family fleeing the Dust Bowl in a VW. Luckily, it was downhill from San Jose to Puntarenas. I remember hoping Rob had souped up the brakes on his rig as well.

But there was no time to think about anything but survival after we left the curb. In this country we just aren't used to operating at the driving intensity level most of the rest of the world employs. I've never heard why this is so. There must be some rational explanation, but for whatever reason, driving in many countries is something akin to a blood sport, and Costa Rica is no exception.

Rob had been doing this awhile, and he was at the top of his game. Now he had a tool to match his abilities. We maneuvered and juked our way to the outskirts of the city, deftly darting and head faking, much like a basketball or soccer player driving toward a goal, judicious use of the horn punctuated by deft heel-and-toe throttle and brake work. It was a masterful performance. There was little conversation; we were in the presence of genius, the perfect blending of man, machine, and opportunity. Although scared nearly stupid, we knew we were fortunate to be witness to this time and place.

And getting out of the city was just a prelude. After leaving San Jose, the highway quickly headed downhill toward the coast, winding and tacking down from the high elevations to sea level, lumbering traffic in both directions requiring a more liberal use of the new horn as Rob swung the steering wheel in graceful arcs as we cut madly through traffic and passed on blind corners, eliciting occasional gasps of appreciation punctuating the muted whining of fear coming from the back seat. He was having a ball.

And it was getting hotter and more humid as we lost altitude, stifling in fact, and that, coupled with the jerking and swaying of our riotous ride down the mountain, made for some copious sweating and no small discomfort. We got to Puntarenas none too soon. I have never been prone to carsickness before or since, but that was a near thing.

The End of the Road

If San Jose was the *City of Springtime*, then Puntarenas must have been the *City of Fetid Late Summer Low Tide Dog Days*, or worse. What a dump. A diesel stained and dirty port town, it oozed heat and stink and humidity, with tired-looking, scabrous dogs slinking around the dingy alleyways on either side of our mud-streaked hotel in the center of town. Rob and Mary said it had been this way as long as anyone could remember: a sad and dangerous place. They usually stayed on the highway and avoided downtown on their way past. They tried to talk us into continuing with them to their place

131

at Drake Bay, and it was tempting the way they described it: a beautiful jungle lodge surrounded by forests full of parrots and monkeys. But that would be for a later time. For now, we had an appointment with the dive boat folks; they were meeting us at our hotel the next morning to transport us to the Okeanos.

The hotel had a worn, dingy look, but no problemas…we'd seen worse. We unloaded our gear and packed it into the lobby, bidding thanks and goodbyes to Rob and Mary, their new horn tootling a lively tune as they drove away. What wonderful characters, real adventurers, I knew their lodge was going to be a great success.

After getting settled in, we wandered around town a bit, picking up some canned goods and produce, and dropped by the Puntarenas Yacht Club for a beverage. The club was located on the estuary side of town (Puntarenas being situated on a long sand spit, the ocean to the south, the river and estuary on the north). Since the tide was going out, we had a great view of all of the garbage that had accumulated up stream over the last day being flushed out past our table. What a great and varied collection of trash, including the swollen bodies of some unfortunate livestock. We declined the appetizer plate, thank you, but enjoyed the view, the clientele, and the huge iguana hissing and posing on the dock.

Like many similar spots all over the world, this yacht club was a temporary stopping-off place for the transient sailing crowd, those hardy souls from nearly every part of the globe who eke their way from port to port, needing an engine part here, scrounging a lost hull fitting there, often waiting for money to be wired from home; it is a unique international culture of its own. And a real eye-opener for those with romantic notions of sailing around the world, it can be a pretty Spartan existence. But it is always a fascinating bunch of characters, and the crowd at Puntarenas was no exception. There were even a couple of treasure hunters who had made their way here, armed with shovels and secret maps, begging for a ride to Cocos Island, but, so far, no one was biting.

We talked with a Swiss couple who had actually recently been out at Cocos Island with their little sailboat. They had gone ashore only briefly for fresh water, they said, and the landing was difficult. But they went on at some length about how beautiful and rugged the place was, hundreds of waterfalls and thick foliage. But it sounded a bit daunting for camping. We'd find out.

A Diverse Community

The van from the dive boat was on schedule the next morning, and it turned out that several of the other clients who were to be joining us on the trip had been staying at the same hotel, a couple from the Midwest and a guy from New York. I could tell they were into their sport; they were comparing notes on all of the upscale dive spots they had visited, and they name-dropped all of the latest equipment brands. Wow. Flip and I exchanged glances. We were going to be a bit behind the curve here; we hadn't even looked at our new dive computer yet, much less the other gear, and I had no idea what the others were talking about when they were discussing all of their new equipment. The dive master, the guy who was going to be in charge of the diving, hopped out of the van and introduced himself; he was a young California kid named Jay, and he seemed friendly and capable, so far so good. Nobody seemed to have recognized Flip yet, and we were hoping it could stay that way.

We didn't start to get strange looks from the others until we started piling our boxes of camping gear and food into the back; that's when Jay blew our cover, explaining to everyone our whole project and *National Geographic* connection. Then, of course, the questions started, everyone commenting on a favorite story they had seen of Flip's in the magazine. So now the pressure was on; trying not to publicly embarrass ourselves in the diving department.

We swung down to the town dock where the tender was waiting to pick us up; we could see the *Okeanos* anchored just offshore. It was a great looking little ship, 100 feet or so long, and looked inviting swinging there at anchor. As we motored closer, we could see the crew lined up along the rail waiting to help us aboard, along with the rest of the passengers, about a dozen people in all. We were the last of the group to arrive, Jay informed us. The crew had gotten fuel and supplies already, so as soon as we got aboard we'd be ready to take off.

This was going to be great. I was used to being on the other side of the hospitality equation, so being a passenger instead of a crewmember held enormous appeal for me, and I couldn't wait. Flip claimed I may have temporarily forgotten my assistant status in my zeal to appreciate this, and that could well have been true. I was enjoying myself already.

Of course our cover was well and truly blown shortly after we came aboard, with everyone making introductions and asking Flip photography questions, but that was okay; there wasn't any way of keeping our mission a secret for long anyway.

All at Sea

We got sorted out and stashed our stuff in our diving lockers on deck and moved into our staterooms down below as the ship pulled anchor, then headed up to the lounge for a briefing and to get to know our fellow shipmates as we headed out.

Now it should be said here that in the past I had always harbored a certain snobbish curiosity about the so-called sport of recreational diving. Maybe it was because we had done all of our diving with ratty equipment and beat up tanks and I was jealous. But it had always seemed to me that merely putting on all the fancy new gear and overcoming the fear of breathing underwater didn't qualify this pastime as a sport. Not like say hockey, for example. You can't just put on the uniform, grab a stick, show up at the rink, and call yourself a hockey player. Maybe it was closer to the sport of bicycling. In bicycling, granted, it was important to put on the silly outfit and the goofy helmet. But then to qualify as a real bicycle sportsman you also had to actually pedal yourself around, engage in competitions, reach for inner strength to surpass your personal best, that kind of thing. Otherwise, you were just posing.

Maybe that was what bothered me; it didn't seem there was anything really required of a sport diver but to sink to the bottom and continue breathing and looking good. Of course there were lots of neat things to see, and you had the option to move around down there if you wanted and pick stuff up. You also had to pay attention to how long you were down and how much air you had left and such, but there wasn't much else required of you. But I also had to admit it was a great excuse to go to interesting places; maybe that was the main attraction of it. Anyway, I was determined to put aside my prejudices. In fact, as I mentioned, it had been awhile since either of us had done much scuba diving, so far from feeling superior at the moment, we were just hoping to blend in and get back into this kind of diving.

As we got to know our fellow shipmates, I gathered that these trips were as much about the social aspects of the journey as about the diving. There were two other couples who had done a number of similar trips together, and three Canadian guys who planned annual dive adventures and were old pros at this kind of thing. And the Costa Rican crew was great, professional, and friendly. The captain and I even had some mutual friends in Panama, and he let us hang out in the bridge for much of the trip. This was turning into a pleasant boat ride.

Mealtimes were lively storytelling sessions, comparing notes on various dive spots and adventures, and in the storytelling department, we were able to hold our own, so far so good. But, as we neared the island, it occurred to us that we were going to have to actually put on our new gear and get in the water, and we actually hadn't even figured out how to use the new dive computer. That night, we broke it out to look it over, but were dismayed to see that the primary instructions were contained on a videocassette we had no immediate means of viewing. There was a quick reference guide card and that would have to suffice. I thought I saw Flip crossing himself. I hadn't suspected he had any particular religious tendencies, but maybe it was just a reflex; I didn't ask him about it.

Isla Nublar

The next afternoon, Jay brought us all up on deck to see the first indication that we were nearing Cocos, a huge pile of clouds over a thin green smudge on the horizon. Everyone stayed to watch the island come into view, frigate birds and booby birds now following the boat in abundance.

As we got closer, we could start to make out details of the island, rugged cliffs and hundreds of waterfalls streaming out of the clouds, what a sight. Another vision, King Kong's Island, came unbidden to mind, and I found myself straining to see signs of a huge gorilla in the steamy valleys.

We circled the entire island; it was about five miles long and an equal distance wide. And it was breathtaking; stark rock formations rising from dense jungle, ragged clouds blowing across white ribbons of water falling from great heights, flocks of white birds wheeling against the green backdrop, beautiful. But it did look rugged; waves crashed against the shore in an almost unbroken line. There were only a couple of places where any kind of landing looked even possible; two bays, Chatham and Wafer, and even they didn't look that hospitable for getting a boat in.

We didn't have any immediate plans for going ashore, however; the boat's plan was to drop anchor in one of the bays and begin diving the next morning. There wasn't much protection from the swells, but it looked like Chatham Bay on the north side was the calmest for the moment, so that's where we went, tucking in next to a couple of big rocks.

An Isolated Case

After we got securely anchored and shut down, the crew launched the skiff, and we took turns riding along the shore of the bay. It was a cool place. Big caves opened unexpectedly along the waterline below thick green jungle, palm trees were dropping coconuts into the surf, and on one small cliff above a small stream you

137

could make out the carved names of ships and dates, many dates indicating the 1800's and a even a couple dating back to the 1700's. Unreal. It looked like a stage set for a pirate movie.

The fishing seemed effortless; the crew trolled a couple of lines around one of the offshore rocks and came back twenty minutes later with a nice Wahoo for dinner.

That evening, as the sun went down, we all gravitated to the upper deck for what would become our evening ritual, the incredible nightly show. Being 300 miles offshore made for no interfering background light, and the stars seemed to pop out in three dimensions in staggering numbers overhead, the Milky Way a bright wash of glowing foam splashed across the sky, the Southern Cross burning on the horizon; it was mesmerizing. The view was accompanied by a gentle, plant-scented breeze and the sound of surf from the unseen island a few hundred yards away as we rocked rhythmically at anchor. Pretty nice.

Like Riding a Wet Bicycle

The next morning, everyone was up early, refreshed and ready. Jay had the group gathered on the back deck soon after breakfast for our final briefing and suit-up before the first dive. We were going to start with an easy one, logically; we would do a shallow exploration of our immediate area, getting our equipment tuned up and getting used to the routine. Good news for us, of course, we weren't anxious to dive into the deep end yet, so to speak. Tanks and weights were distributed, gear was pulled from diving lockers and donned, and what a resplendent bunch we were. Looking around, I was thankful Flip had us upgrade our gear. I could never have imagined such a shiny and colorful collection of divers. Everyone had gewgaws and gadgets galore, bright strap-on knives and tools, sparkling octopus regulators and dials, and dive computers and suits of every color and stripe. The couples of course were in matching outfits. It looked like a school of parrot fish prepped for Mardi gras or some gay astronaut convention. We weren't nearly as resplendent as the others, but at least we didn't look like the poor drab relations we would have looked like in our old gear.

The whole bunch of us hit the water, and the good news was that all of our new stuff worked great, no embarrassing equipment malfunctions; in fact, we fit right in, like we knew what we were doing. And the dive computer was moron-proof, had big display numbers, and was simple to use. What a relief. I'm pretty sure Flip felt the same way. As I mentioned, it had been awhile, but it all came back like we had just been diving yesterday.

As a bonus, just as we were climbing back aboard a huge manta ray came sailing in out of the deep and made several passes around the boat before taking off again, this was just getting better and better.

We made several more dives that first day, exploring the rocks and reefs by the anchorage, going a little deeper each dive, a great variety of reef fish and sea life in evidence. We were ready for the bigger stuff.

The next morning the boat repositioned south to a new spot, a submerged rock a short distance offshore that was alive with reef fish, moray eels, and slipper lobsters, and was reputedly a good place to spot the giant whale sharks that were common these parts. No whale shark this day, but what a fascinating collection of undersea life, every dive turning up something new. And the next day was billed as the most exciting yet; we were finally going to the Shark Place.

The Reformed School

Early that next morning we motored over to the west side of the island, out past the ranger station in Wafer Bay. As we went by, Flip and I peered anxiously through the binoculars at what was soon to be our home. It wasn't much, just a shack with a big radio antenna, but it looked like it was situated on the only flat bit of land we'd seen here so far, so at least we wouldn't have to camp clinging to the side of a cliff. But we would deal with that tomorrow, for now we were approaching our destination.

It was called Piedra Sucia, or Dirty Rock, maybe because of all of the bird guano covering it, but we didn't care what it looked like above water. Everyone was more interested in what was underneath. Sharks. Lots of them. Hundreds, supposedly. They weren't always there, but it happened often enough that there was a better than even chance.

After we dropped anchor, Jay took a quick reconnoiter underwater and came back with the news that there were indeed sharks, hammerheads, and not just a few. We were in luck.

Talk about excited. Everybody checked and double-checked their equipment and their cameras, obviously a bit nervous at the prospect of the upcoming interaction. These were big hammerhead sharks, after all, and there was a certain natural reluctance to jumping into the water knowing they were there. And not just based on popular opinion, multiple viewings of *Jaws* and a fondness for the Discovery Channel and the like. There was also a deep-seated aversion based upon millennia of evolution, all the way back to the preference of our dim progenitors to not become bait.

We all slipped into the water and sure enough, there was a huge school of milling hammerheads. Initially, everyone stayed close just under the surface, like any respectable group of prey, the idea being that if you stayed near the middle they'd get your buddies first. But it became evident that the sharks had no interest in us; they were just going about whatever business was at hand, so the group spread out and headed down.

A big hammerhead swung over in our direction, and it struck me how weird-looking, almost comical, they were, with eyes bulging out at the end of big stalks growing from the side of their heads, and the crescent mouth in a permanent inverted frown. I was carrying several camera housings, and as he came closer, Flip was changing out different cameras, snapping furiously. Finally it was evident the shark was coming right for us, so he ended up eyeball to eyeball with the thing with the widest angle lens possible.

The monster finally finned languidly away, seemingly not as impressed with us as we were with him.

Looking down, we could see big groups of hammerheads milling around several small sea mounds, so we headed down to have a look. As we got closer, we could see that these were cleaning stations, where the sharks would come to get the little parasites and growths cleaned from their gills by the little wrasses and reef fish that made the mounds their home. What a great system. Like the fawning populace with an invading army, opportunistically trading services in exchange for profit and protection, these little guys were cleaning away, darting in and out of the shark's gills and mouths. And the sharks were actually lining up, like servicemen at the working-girl cribs on Honolulu's Hotel Street, to take their turn. It was fascinating. We went from mound to mound; it was a vast system, and Flip was getting lots of great shots.

Soon, it was time to begin thinking about heading back. We had been down deep enough and long enough that we'd need to do a brief decompression stop before heading to the surface, and the boat's anchor chain was the preferred spot to do that, so we started gathering up our gear. But conditions had changed. The current had picked up from the opposite direction from when we set out, and visibility had decreased, so we took a moment to get our bearings.

We were pretty sure about the way back to the boat and had a rough compass direction, so we headed off. There was a moment of doubt; we thought we should be able to see the boat on the surface by now, but there was no sign of it. We exchanged looks and shrugs. This was the screwing-up-fear we had harbored. We didn't feel we were in any danger, we were confident the boat crew would pick us up wherever we surfaced, and we had all been issued an emergency signaling device, a brightly-colored inflatable tube the diver could trigger and wave from the surface if they needed to be picked up. There was scarcely a dive went by without somebody getting disoriented and having to inflate their big tube (Weenie-of-Shame the group called it) as a signal to come fetch them in the skiff. But we didn't want to be the ones to have to do that; we were supposed to be professionals.

About this time we heard a boat motor approaching, a different sound from our skiff, and we watched as a boat trail soared high over our heads and disappeared. It could be only one thing, a boat from the ranger station heading to our anchored ship, so we were in luck. We had a trail pointing directly home. We were close; we swam another twenty yards, and the boat came into view. As we hung off the chain, we heard the skiff from our boat being launched several times to pick up other hapless members of our party who had gotten disoriented by the changing conditions, and there we dangled, smug in the there-but-for-the-grace-of-God knowledge that we'd undeservedly dodged an embarrassment. Still, it felt good. Maybe there was more skill involved with this sport diving business than I'd given it credit for. Or luck.

By the time we got back aboard, the park rangers had left, but it seemed that they had come out to check on us. They had received word by radio that there would be a couple of people coming ashore to camp on the island for a while, and they were following up. We were scheduled to go ashore the next day, and they had left instructions and advice on the best landing place, the only landing place, a small channel in the beach in front of the station.

Maroonic Behavior

We stowed our dive gear, got our camping gear and boxes of food together, and prepared to be transported to the island the next morning. The cook augmented our provisions with a few treats from the galley, and we had a last civilized goodbye meal aboard with our new friends and shipmates. When the *Okeanos* returned (theoretically) in a few days to pick us up, it would be with a new group of divers, a new audience for our stories anyway. We pressed upon the crew several times the importance and the absolute necessity of their return, regardless of whatever might transpire ashore, whether it be mechanical problems or Armageddon, or a plague of frogs, or whatever; we made them promise they'd come back. There may have been a slight manic edge to our repeated entreaties; they began to edge away when we brought it up. So then of course we had to laugh it off, but five minutes later it would come unbidden, "But, *really*, you do need to be sure you come back...." I'm sure it was tiresome.

Bright and early the next morning we made landfall, Jay running us in with the skiff to the small notch in the beach the rangers had indicated, where we quickly unloaded our supplies on to shore. We reaffirmed the pickup time and date (again), then got Jay turned around and headed back, leaving us with the sudden realization that now we were well and truly committed to Cocos.

We could see the ranger's inflatable boat where they stored it in a small lagoon on the other side of the beach; they apparently manhandled it across the low spot when they needed to venture out, no small feat even at high tide. I had new respect for the mysterious rangers we had yet to meet.

We long-shored our stuff up into the clearing by the ranger station and found the place empty, but there was a note on the door left for us. They had gone to the other side of the island for the day on some project or another, but they had cleared out a place under a dilapidated thatch-covered lean-to shed at the edge of the clearing for us to stay. And there was a list of rules, among them the necessity to use the outhouse behind the station for our toilet, directions to the garbage pit, and instructions for us to use the fresh water pipe rigged up behind the lean-to for our water and washing needs. I got the impression they weren't accustomed to hosting guests.

We moved our gear over to the shed and set up our little camp, sweeping the dirt floor smooth and laying out the cooking and sleeping areas. We hung our food in a bag from one of the overhead poles to discourage whatever critters might be tempted to steal it. Good thing, too, judging by the number of pig tracks we saw around the area later.

It took us most of the day to get squared away, and by the time the rangers returned we were preparing our first meal of our adventure, a real gourmet treat, and one that would be repeated almost nightly. It consisted of a big handful of pasta boiled up in our big pot, clumsily drained, and augmented by canned sauce and numerous chunks of dry salami carved off one of the numerous sticks we'd brought, and liberally sprinkled with dry Parmesan cheese flakes. A side salad of lettuce and cabbage doused with oil and vinegar made the feast complete. But it was evident immediately that we had forgotten a vital camp tool, a colander for draining the pasta, and that was the subject of our first and last request from the newly arrived rangers.

In retrospect, a request to borrow a colander is probably not the safest of conversational ground with which to start a relationship with someone with whom you don't share a common language. But it seemed important at the time.

There were three of them, they straggled into camp just as we were starting into dinner, and they were a rough-looking bunch. The big bearded guy, who resembled Che Guevara, was the leader; the others deferred to him when, after initial pleasantries, we struggled in rudimentary Spanish with our request to borrow a colander, deferentially communicating the desire for the thing with holes with which to get pasta from water separate. That set the tone right there; we didn't have much interaction with them after that. I got the impression they weren't that excited about having people staying on the island anyway, especially ones that appeared a little nuts. And apparently they didn't have a colander.

They didn't seem to be that happy a collection of rangers anyway. We speculated upon whether there might possibly have been some troublesome *Lord of the Flies* interaction business going on. But, for whatever reason, we saw them only occasionally during the rest of our time there, which was fine with us; they seemed a little serious.

Remarking upon our Territory

The next morning we set out exploring. We had a map that showed several trails snaking across the island, a couple leading to the tops of the two main peaks, and one shorter one connecting the two bays, Wafer, where we were, and Chatham, the place we had initially anchored. We chose to head over to Chatham because it seemed like an easy warm-up.

I had another reason to want to get over to Chatham. When I had been doing my research, I had come across a description of the treasure cache of one of the largest of the reputed treasures, the Loot of Lima, reportedly buried near Chatham Bay. It was in a passage I had copied down left by a certain Captain Thompson, describing the location of the buried loot, and it read as follows:

"Once at the bay, follow the coastline 'till you find a creek, where, at high water mark, you go up the bed of a stream which flows inland. Now you step out 70 paces, west by south, and against the skyline you will see a gap in the hills. From any other point, the gap is invisible. Turn north, and walk to a stream. You

will now see a rock with a smooth face, rising sheer like a cliff. At the height of a man's shoulder, above the ground, you will see a hole large enough for you to insert your thumb. Thrust in an iron bar, twist it 'round in the cavity, and behind you will find a door which opens on the treasure."

Those pesky pirates. There was also some talk about booby traps and deadfalls and other discouragements for would-be treasure seekers; it was fascinating. Sort of an *Indiana Jones* meets *Pirates of the Caribbean* setup. Of course, I didn't really think I had a chance of stumbling across a fortune in pirate booty. That was as ridiculous as thinking lottery tickets were a good investment, but who wouldn't be intrigued? Anyway, I had brought a copy of Captain Thompson's instructions with me, just in case.

It soon became clear that hiking around Cocos Island wasn't anybody's idea of a walk in the park, national designation or no. It was incredibly dense foliage, and muddy, slippery and stifling, unpleasant hiking for the most part, mostly following pig trails. We slogged and panted our way up and over to the next bay, slipping on rocks and clutching at vines, nothing resembling a blue lagoon in sight. We did have a couple of brief vistas from the top, but mostly it was a dank and shadowy slog. We found the stream that we had seen from the boat that first day, and there were many more carved dates and ship names in the rocks along its banks; it must have been a popular fresh water gathering spot. What a sense of history, to think of all those sailors of long ago who stood on that spot and took the time to etch their existence into this rock. What was the manner of the shipboard life they were living in the 1700's? Likely not that pleasant. Most of us would probably want our money back from that cruise.

Of course I was intently looking for gaps in the hills and thumb-sized holes in cliff faces, just in case, but I wasn't having any luck. The treasure was probably going to be safe from us.

Deep in the Heart...of Darkness

We explored along the small beach in Chatham for a while, just enjoying being out of the humidity and claustrophobia of the underbrush for a while. When we finally started back, it was again impossible to see much of anything in the thick undergrowth; those pirates must have been a tough bunch. (But I guess that goes without saying...) As we slipped and struggled along a rocky ridge leading back across to Wafer, it was clear to me how easy it would be to simply be swallowed up by Cocos Island. Both sides of the ridge fell away into dense foliage, dark and impenetrable, and we could occasionally hear feral pigs snuffling around down below. We never got a good look at one, but heard them rooting around constantly. I shuddered to think what would happen to anyone who fell down into one of those dark ravines.

I recalled now a grim bit of history I had uncovered when I was researching Cocos: the shameful episode of the Polynesian ex-slaves who had been abandoned here in 1863. Apparently, the slaves, who had been conscripted from their South Seas home on an earlier adventure, had proven to be unsuitable, perhaps ill, and so arrangements were made to transport them back home. The ship *Adelante* was hired to do the job, but it didn't follow through. Apparently, the lazy captain, encountering Cocos Island enroute and probably figuring that an island is an island, and these were islanders after all (and it was a lot closer than the South Seas), dumped all 426 captives off here and continued on his way. When the survivors were picked up by the vessel *Tumbes* that happened to stop by for water a month later, there were only thirty-eight left. What unimaginable horror they must have endured. Such stories of inhumanity are so common in our history that they scarcely warrant a footnote. It doesn't bode well for our "Species of the Millennium" award.

With these happy thoughts in mind, we straggled back to our little camp to clean up and prepare another feast, a little chastened by our first foray out into the wild. We didn't know what the rangers were having for dinner (we could see a light on in their shack, but they didn't venture out). But for us, we had overcome our lack of a colander with a complicated lid positioning technique that produced perfectly drained pasta every time. It was a two-man operation, the lid-man, (or *lidador*) deftly checking the glob of pasta in the pot before it spilled out onto the ground as the water was poured out. We had finally mastered it, so all was good. We were surviving quite well despite our equipment shortcomings, thank you.

Taking the Plunge

The next day we decided to tackle the trek to the first peak to our north; there was supposed to be the remains of a wrecked WWII airplane up there (isn't that required of any self-respecting uninhabited island?).

We were better prepared after the previous day's excursion; we packed light and brought plenty of energy bars and not so much in the way of camera equipment. You needed both arms free to navigate through this terrain, at least one to keep wiping the sweat out of your eyes; it was muggy.

We did find the remains of the downed plane; it was a B-24 that had crashed on its way to Galapagos during WWII, with no reported survivors. Besides scattered junk, the only things recognizable were a couple of propellers sticking up out of the jungle. You had to wonder about the circumstances of the crash, why they chose to ditch into the mountain instead of the water, and what was going on in their final moments. More mysteries we'd never solve...more human remains ingested by the island.

On the way back down, part of the trail ran along a stream filled with deep pools, and I made a misstep and ended up tumbling into one. I managed to get my pack off and above water quickly, but not before submerging part of it; the part carrying Flip's flash unit. Bad assistant. We didn't have a replacement. But at least I was marginally cleaner.

When we got back to camp, we disassembled the flash and got the circuit boards and wires spread out to dry before we tried to power it up again. I felt terrible; Flip could really use the flash for fill light in these shadowy conditions (he not-so-subtly made it clear), and it was imperative we get it working if we were to have any chance of getting a nighttime shot of marauding pigs, so we were hoping for the best.

A Shell of a Pet

The next day we elected to take it easy and give the flash unit pieces a chance to dry thoroughly in the sun, so it was a good opportunity to explore the immediate area. And to give Flip a little alone time in which to contemplate the dismal specter of living without a flash strobe for a couple of days.

As I was exploring the beach in front of our camp, I saw a shell purposefully making its way along shore, and making pretty good time, too. When I picked it up, I could see that it was a little hermit crab, one of

150

those opportunistic squatters that make old cast-off shells their temporary homes, carrying their shelter along like homeless people living in their cars. He was a cute little guy. When he tried to grab my thumb with his claw, I named him Thomas Pynchon (I was reading one of his books at the time) and decided to take him home as a pet. Every camp needs a mascot, and now he was it. I put him in an old crate that was lying around and fed him some salami, which he seemed to like. I could just imagine the alien abduction stories he'd be able to tell his friends later. I was becoming easily amused.

That afternoon, we put the flash unit back together, put in new batteries, and fired it off. It worked perfectly. All was right with the world; we'd dodged another bullet.

Assault on the Iglesias

We made preparations for the trip to the highest spot on the island, Mount Iglesias, a peak over 2000 feet high, just because it was there.

We started early, and it was a tough, sweaty, grueling trudge up into the cloud forest, around four slippery miles from camp to the top. What a great view from up there though; it cleared momentarily just as we reached the top. You got a real sense of the isolation of this place looking out at the vast expanse of ocean in every direction.

But then something happened on the way down I will never forget. We were hiking along a level spot, the forest thinning somewhat as we came around a corner, and hovering there suddenly, directly in my path, in a brilliant shaft of sunlight with dust motes swirling around it, was a vision of supreme loveliness. I learned later the bird is called a fairy tern, and I can't imagine a more apt name. It was surreal, pure white, perfect, with a shiny obsidian black eye regarding me, suspended and ethereal. And then it was gone, just an afterimage of beauty remaining. If primitive man needed an angel, or a celestial manifestation of the possibility of perfection, then this was the ticket. Wow. That image remains vivid to this day.

Reentry

We had accomplished pretty much what we had set out to do, to explore and get a sense of Cocos Island, and now we began to break camp and prepare to meet the *Okeanos* at our assigned time the next day for our trip back.

The afternoon before we left I had some free time, so I walked down to a little beach I hadn't visited before, a little way past our camp, little realizing I was about to experience a disturbing epiphany, one that was quite the opposite from my earlier encounter with the fairy tern.

I sat down on a rock in front of a beach entirely composed of small shells; it seemed like a peaceful place to contemplate the serene nature of this place. But as I sat there, I became aware of a rustling, muted clicking or buzzing sound, seemingly coming from all around me. And then I noticed that the shells were all alive and moving, seemingly thousands of them. They were everywhere, even in the branches of the trees next to me; they were hermit crabs, like our little mascot back at the camp. I could see their legs now, all different sizes and colors. And they were congregating around a large mound in front of me. The horde parted for a moment, and I could see that the mound was something organic, something that had been dead for some time. They were eating it.

I had a sudden vision that the whole island was alive, the crabs, the pigs, the intense greenery. Life was so intense and focused here that constant vigilance was necessary to avoid being consumed. It wasn't a particularly malevolent feeling, like the place didn't harbor me any ill will, but it was clear that if I didn't pay attention it would happily eat me, like it ate the hapless slaves who had been dropped off here, like it ate the crew of that airplane.

Shuddering, I returned to the sunlight. I would have to bring our little camp-mate back to this place; he was missing out on the action.

As I gave the little hermit crab his freedom and watched him scuttle away, I was struck by another, more benign vision: my returning to this place someday. Just as had happened with a grown Elsa the lion cub bounding back from her new life in the wild in *Born Free* to greet her old benefactor George Adamson with affectionate recognition, I saw Thomas Pynchon, dominant and larger now (due in large part to the advantage of an early salami diet), sleek and glossy in his new Giant Cowry shell, emerging from the sea to greet me, his little eye stalks gleaming in recognition. The small remaining part of me still sane knew it was definitely time to leave.

Reflective Glare

And so we left. Jay was there right on schedule to pick us up as we bid goodbye to our friendly rangers, who waved back, obviously happy to see us go. (I hoped they'd be OK and wouldn't get eaten, or eat each other.) It felt wonderful to be back in the bosom of comfortable shipboard life, with a new crew of friendly divers, and the leisure of a comfortable sea voyage home. When we motored away, sitting up on deck in the sun, watching

Cocos Island recede to invisibility in our wake, there was time to process the experience we had just had.

For my part, as I reflected upon pirates and slaves, and fairy terns and hermit crabs, it came to me that life is equally capable of manifesting both acts of beastly horror and expressions of sublime grace and beauty. (Tedious I know. But I don't reflect often.) And a question presented itself: could the outcome be a matter of choice, or just circumstance, or a combination of both? A lot to think about in one morning. Or indeed in one lifetime. But, for now, I was getting hungry, and I idly wondered what was for lunch.

But there was another more tenacious thing that still haunted me: The existential glimpse I had at the crab beach of the implacable engine of life manifesting itself from the howling void; the clacking, killing, eating, struggling, breeding...*the relentless desire to prevail*...that was unnerving. Like the implacable will that drives silicone-based life forms to ooze their way into existence as machines of grim competition around searing black smoking deep sea vents. Or the kind of glimpse that could have led a T.S. Eliot to envision himself as "a pair of ragged claws scuttling across the floors of silent seas." That kind of vision, to those of us of little faith, of the planet resolutely becoming aware of itself, of matter becoming animate, is disturbing, even horrifying. And it brings up deep-seated questions of what and how and, most disturbing, *why*. And where was lunch? Cocos Island had been an exhausting experience on several levels.

For my part, my small overwhelmed soul was in desperate need of three things: 1) a thorough binging on a big bag of comfort fast food, 2) a long luxuriating session in a downtown massage parlor, and 3) a marathon round of Disney animated movies involving cute forest animals, not necessarily in that order. I couldn't wait to get back to civilization.

Chasing the Blues Away in Panama

The Wild Blue Down Yonder

I'm not sure what we were thinking, looking back on it. But this trip seemed like a perfectly reasonable idea at the time.

We had been hearing stories for a couple of years from Jim Darling and other researchers about alleged blue whale sightings off the coast of Central America back in the late 1980's, and that was a big deal back then. Blue whale sightings were much rarer in those days than they are now. For example, in my case up to then I'd only had a glimpse once of a solitary blue in Sri Lanka, and I remember being amazed by how huge it was compared to the whales we were used to seeing. I wanted to see another one.

In the meantime, Flip's earlier Humpback and other whale stories for *National Geographic* magazine had been getting a lot of attention; he had published some groundbreaking stuff, and his career was taking off. He was gaining the reputation as the premier whale-picture-guy at the magazine, and a blue whale photo would be a coup, so he was equally anxious to find one.

The problem in this case was that there was no organized blue whale research effort going on down in

Central America at the time, only the occasional sighting by a vessel passing by, or a report from someone who happened to spot one in the course of looking for something else. But there were enough reports that it seemed worth the gamble to have a look.

It was risky for a couple of reasons, though. For one thing, there were some rumblings of political unrest going on down there (but I'd spent a lot of time there recently, and we figured at the time that this was nothing new...). For another, all of the previous stories Flip had done had been accomplished by joining up with some established research group or other who already had a good idea where their target animals might reliably be found. In this case, we'd be on our own, covering a lot of ocean, Ahab-like, hoping to spot a whale. But Flip figured it would be worth a try, so he put a request in to the magazine for a small stipend to mount a preliminary expedition to go down there to have a look. And, to their credit, they agreed—he got the go-ahead.

Now I feel in fairness it should be stated here, to defuse any false hopes a reader may entertain that this story might actually lead to some kind of whale encounter, that indeed *no cetaceans were even slightly disturbed in the pursuit of this story.* If you are looking for accounts of whale interactions, this chapter isn't the place. We didn't find them. Sometimes that happens, and it only seems fair to make that clear right from the outset. The only whale we even got a glimpse of during this whole zany fiasco was some weird beaked whale I'd never even heard of, and him only for a second. But in this case, the trip turned out to be quite an adventure anyway.

We started out full of high hopes. As I mentioned, I had been working down in Panama the previous few years running a ship for Exploration Cruise

Lines, so I had a few contacts down there to help put this together, and I immediately started putting out feelers to locate a boat for our trip. We figured a small yacht would suffice for our needs, with a minimal crew in addition to the two of us and two lovely others; my then-girlfriend-now-wife Cherie and Flip's friend Kathy, as assistants. (In my case, assistant to the assistant.) It goes without saying that I was looking forward to this.

The Need for Consuling

My friend Pancho, a Panamanian-American who lived there (and who was, among many other things, a vice-consul at the American embassy), responded almost immediately that he had the perfect boat in mind. He had already tentatively reserved it; it would be waiting for us. Now it must be said that Pancho's advice had to be treated with some care. He was one of those guys who are great fun to be around and up for anything, but he didn't seem to be bound by the same rules as everybody else. I didn't even want to know about all of the stuff he was up to. But, in this case, he had sent the details and pictures of the yacht he had arranged for us, and it looked perfect, so we put aside any misgivings we had and told him to book it.

The last time I had seen Pancho was the year before when he had dragged me along to the famous Panamanian horse races.

He had a friend who owned some of the horses running that day, and who had a private box at the track. We roared up to the gate in his fancy Mercedes, him waving his diplomatic passport out the window at the guards as usual, guaranteeing us a front row parking spot and royal treatment. While I was sitting up in that box that day, rum and Coke in one hand and a fistful of winning tickets in the other (somehow the people in that

158

box always seemed to know which horses were going to win), I had a troubling premonition. Looking out at the thousands of betting fans in the stands (who unlike us didn't know which horses were going to win, and would likely be a little upset if they knew that we knew), I had a vision of the masses rising up as one to scale the walls and slay the corrupt upper classes (which in this case included us in the box) when they figured out what was going on. My vision wasn't too far off looking back at the way things were going to turn out down here soon.

But for the present, we were here for a simple yacht trip in search of whales, no political agendas and hopefully no complications. But it couldn't be that simple.

General Alarm

We had an uneventful flight in to Panama City. Pancho had sent word that he would temporarily be on the other side of the country on business when we arrived, but he had arranged for one of the agency guys to meet us at the airport to take us to our hotel and then to go see the boat. He would meet us later at his fancy private club for dinner that night. I was glad to be going back and looking forward to seeing my old friend again.

But things had changed since the last time I had been here. As we were being driven from the airport to our hotel, it was evident from the action on the streets that popular opinion was turning decidedly against the long-standing regime of General Noriega and his gang. There was anti-government graffiti everywhere and some sign-carrying demonstrations taking place downtown. Our driver told us that there had recently been a bogus popular election that had clearly been rigged by the general, and there was a resulting public outrage; people had finally had enough, he said.

Noriega was bad news; even in my short history there, I had met a number of people who had foul dealings with his bunch. One was an attractive young Belgian woman who, while working at her country's Panamanian embassy, had encountered the general, who had apparently taken a fancy to her. When she rebuffed his amorous advances, she had subsequently been so hounded by his minions she had to leave the country. I had spent an uncomfortable dinner with her one night shortly before she left watching unmarked cars with tinted windows cruise slowly past our street-side restaurant table in Panama City; it was scary and pretty much ruined dessert. I was worried for her and glad when I heard she'd gotten away. Those guys were capable of nasty behavior.

The upshot of all of this was that our timing for this adventure didn't look like the best political-climate-wise, but we figured these kinds of things had happened here before, and, if we just kept our heads down and went about our business, we should be able to avoid any problems. Right.

Yachts of Questions

The yacht looked great when we got to the marina. It wasn't new, but it was tidy-looking and had a couple of nice staterooms set up for us. The captain and deckhand were off getting supplies, but we would meet with them the following morning.

We got settled in to our hotel and got ready for our fancy dinner engagement. Private clubs such as the one Pancho had invited us to seem to be a common fixture in many third world countries, remnants from colonial times, opulent and exclusive, the places where the power elite used to gather to socialize and plot the fate of the country away from the hoi polloi and

160

common rabble. These days, they were mostly just snobby vestiges of a former order, but the food in this place was supposed to still be excellent.

Pancho met us at the club with his beautiful Nicaraguan wife Marisa. They made quite a striking couple, him big, ruddy, and blonde, and her dainty and regal, and something of a saint, one of the nicest people I've ever met. How she tolerated Pancho's antics was a mystery that baffled all of us who were their friends, but there you are.

Dinner was of course fantastic, the service and the wait staff impeccable, the normal hilarity taking place among the white linen and the crystal. It was a great evening, with lots of catching up and rehashing of old stories. But when we got around to discussing the yacht, Pancho let it slip that the boat's owner was a close friend and top advisor to General Noriega, just so we'd know to steer our conversation away from political topics when anyone was around. Great. How Pancho had set this up was anybody's guess, but we were committed now, regardless of our feelings about the general.

The Long and Short of it

When we arrived at the boat the next morning, only the captain and deckhand were there stowing gear aboard, and introductions were made. That was fine with me; I had no desire to meet this mysterious owner. But how to describe the crew? Central casting couldn't have done a better job. They were such opposites; they could have been a vaudeville team. Beebee the captain was tall, very dark, and very thin, with thick horned rim glasses perched on the tip of his nose, and a huge smile; he just radiated friendliness. His deckhand Amable (meaning Happy) was short, also very dark, squat, and muscular; he radiated not exactly menace, but certainly not happiness, nor friendliness. I'm not sure I've ever met anyone whose name was at such odds with his character (but now it occurs to me that maybe that was a tongue-in-cheek nickname, like calling a short guy Stretch). Their accents were that delightful Caribbean patois (*Ya mon, bumbo clot...*), although, in truth Beebee did most of the talking for both of them, like Penn and Teller.

Beebee made us feel at home, showing us to our staterooms, Flip and Kathy settling into the main cabin, and Cherie and I taking the V berth up forward. Amable glowered along behind with our gear.

Pancho put in an appearance to see us off (and probably to ease his conscience), insisting that I take along his lucky fishing lure in case we got into any good fishing. It was a battle-scarred resin plug I remembered from a previous fishing trip I'd been on with him, covered with ragged marlin scrapes resembling file marks on every square inch of it, which I reluctantly accepted, knowing how fond he was of it.

The boat appeared to be in good shape mechanically, and on the surface seemed to have most of the necessary navigation gear we would need as well as the necessary charts. For this trip, since we would be spending time offshore, in addition to the usual sextant, I had brought with me one of the new (in those pre-GPS days) Sat Nav sets for determining our position just in case.

We got settled in, Cherie and Kathy organizing the galley and checking inventories, Flip and I getting in their way, checking everything out. There was even a blender, always a good sign.

Beebee and Amable had done a great job of stocking food and supplies. They had obviously done this before, lots of food, fresh fruit, and beverages; we were stocked and ready to go. So, figuring there was no time like the present, we waved our goodbyes to Pancho, and shoved off.

Equipment Malofunctiono

We headed south from the canal and then west (the canal runs north and south, not east and west as one would logically expect), thinking to get up near the Costa Rica border before we headed offshore, the area where most of the blue whale sightings had taken place.

In talking with Captain Beebee, I soon found out that the boat normally didn't travel far from its home base. In fact, all they had ever done with it was the occasional party or short fishing trip out in front of Panama City; they had rarely gone out overnight or far from home and never out of sight of land. Hmm.

And there turned out to be some equipment problems that weren't evident at first glance. The radar only worked out to a distance of about a hundred yards or so, its magnetron was shot, and the magnetic compass was so far off that it was unusable, indicating a direction that was almost completely opposite of the direction we were heading. I couldn't totally blame Beebee for this; he was used to just driving around the home front in good visibility and daylight. But this trip was a little more involved and might require something more in the way of navigation aids.

We got the Sat Nav wired in and set up; we taped the antenna to a broomstick and clamped it onto the mast, and I was now glad that I had brought it. With that position information coming in, we could get the compass adjusted to an acceptable degree and continue with our trip, but I wasn't as happy as I might have been with our new vessel.

But the engines and the other gear seemed to be running fine, and the weather report sounded promising, so theoretically all was well. It felt great to be underway and looking for whales. So far so good.

We weren't out of the shakedown-problem-phase yet, though. Shortly after we got underway, Kathy came running up to the bridge with the report of a waterfall in her stateroom. One of the air conditioning circulation pipes had burst in the overhead, and water was cascading down one wall of their cabin. We soon got that secured, but it meant the end of the air conditioning…in the tropics. At least we hadn't gotten used to it yet.

Prison Pageant

We figured we should probably anchor before it got completely dark, given our unfamiliarity with the region, so we made for the nearest anchorage, Coiba Island—a beautiful place, but also the location of Panama's maximum security prison, where they put the political prisoners and really bad guys; the name struck fear into most Panamanians' hearts. I could tell Beebee and Amable weren't all that excited to be in the neighborhood, but we reluctantly tucked into a beautiful cove a ways off a tidy little beach on the east side of the island and settled in for the night. The first of many very long nights for Beebee and Amable I suspect, looking back on it. They spent this and every subsequent night of our trip up on the flying bridge keeping a watchful eye on the darkness. They even took their meals up there; we didn't really see much of them, even though we tried to include them in our festivities as much as possible. I had the feeling they weren't that comfortable being away from their home territory.

But the rest of us were having a ball. Cherie and Kathy dove into the galley and started throwing together the first of many sumptuous meals while Flip and I started going over our charts and planning our trip. The boat rocked gently at anchor while the daylight faded, and life was good.

After dinner, we all retired to the back deck for a little cool evening air and what was to become our nightly Scrabble game, and we were able to make out a faint glow in the sky from the lights of the prison on the other side of the island. It was sobering; local rumor had it that this was where anyone who disagreed with the current administration went to disappear, and that was probably true. We thought we could make out faint sounds of a sporting event, or a celebration, however, coming occasionally on the breeze, and when someone suggested that it sounded like a pageant, maybe even a Miss Coiba Beauty Pageant, that of course in our minds was what it became.

So, naturally, this line of thinking spiraled out of control. There was some talk of the possible necessity of entering one of our number into the pageant, if we were to be overrun and that were to become required to save the rest of us. (This sort of thing happens when a group like ours is stuck together without sufficient distractions, imaginations come undone.) It didn't stop there. When no volunteers were forthcoming, a vote was taken on the preferred candidate to be offered up, with names put into a hat. When the results were tallied, the winner, to my distress, was me. It was almost unanimous, the only dissenting vote was mine (I'd voted for Flip), so it was obvious even Cherie had turned on me. Ingrates.

I had a restless night. I knew it was only an overwrought fantasy brought on by the heat and overactive imaginations, but I had a nightmare involving prison pageant scouts swarming the shore, and the rest of that villainous bunch giving me up to the mob...they'd do it, too...

Passing the Bar

The next morning dawned clear and calm and beautiful without a soul in sight, just a beautiful island and a white sandy beach, so the talent portion of my routine wouldn't be necessary. We decided that before we crossed the border to Costa Rican waters we would head over to the Panama mainland and up an estuary to the town of Pedregal for some last minute galley supplies and to see if we could repair our air conditioning problem.

The trip into Pedregal seemed daunting when we arrived there that afternoon. I would have been reluctant to try it myself, but Beebee assured us that it was a routine transit undertaken by boats a lot bigger than ours on a regular basis. The entrance to the estuary was a tricky affair, basically running through the breakers across the bar, and then winding a few miles inland to the port, the whole thing subject to shifting sand bars and submerged logs, only to be attempted at high tide and with the assistance of a local pilot. But Beebee knew one of the pilots, so the arrangement was made over the radio for a guy to come out to us in a little panga (the name for the local skiff), and lead us in.

The whole thing worked like clockwork. We could see the brightly painted little panga bouncing out toward us through the surf, and when it reached us it turned about and we fell in behind. We paralleled the beach for a short distance, then darted through the waves toward a line of anchored plastic milk jugs the pilots used to mark the shifting hazards and sand bars.

We made a sinuous trip up around several bends, still following the plastic buoys, heading inland through the dense jungle, until the waterway widened and a respectable sized port, including a small marina, came into view. We headed to the marina transient dock, feeling smug about the whole affair, and began tying up, when disaster struck.

In the Land of the Blind...

As Beebee was leaning over the side of the boat tying off a fender, his glasses slid off his nose into the water and disappeared without a ripple. He stood blinking slowly with that surprised owl-like look very myopic people tend to have without their glasses, an uncharacteristic, mournful expression settling over his features. This wasn't good. It was no use asking if he had a second pair; the look on his face said everything.

We finished tying up in silence, adjusting to this new world where our captain had lost his sight (the thickness of the lenses left little doubt). It was a reserved crew that went about the business of getting the boat secured, checking in, and settling up with the pilot. Everyone treated Beebee delicately, avoiding eye contact, (not that that would have made much difference in the present situation).

The water was dirty here, almost opaque, and the fathometer read about thirty feet under us. If that wasn't bad enough, it was getting dark, and there was a moderate current running through the marina. Flip determined that if we were to have any chance of diving for the glasses, we'd need to do it quickly, before the current changed, and before we completely lost the light.

He tied a light weight onto a piece of fishing line and tossed it over, and it stretched out a ways behind the boat before settling onto the bottom. He grabbed a

167

mask, stripped down to his shorts, and splashed into the dirty water, following the fishing line back and down. He was under what seemed like an inordinately long time before he popped up for air, shaking his head in the negative to let us know he hadn't had any luck. Down he went again, repeating the process several more times, coming up a little farther downstream each time, when finally, when everyone was finally coming to the realization that it was fruitless, his hand popped up holding Beebee's big glasses. A huge cheer went up, not only from us but also from the small crowd that had gathered on the dock to watch the entertainment. I don't think people did a lot of swimming around that port.

Flip clambered back aboard to a grateful Beebee, his smile returning brightly with his dirty specs; it was like popping fresh batteries into a favorite toy. We hosed the toxic mud off Flip and sent him below to shower. He had taken one for the team, and we were grateful and hoped he wouldn't come down with some horrible disease or chemical lesions from that nasty water. Yuck. But our captain could see again, which was a good thing.

Offshore Grilling

The next morning we were not only able to get all of the galley supplies we needed in that little port town, but we also topped off our fuel and found the fitting we needed to fix the air conditioning; things were just getting better and better. Around noon when the tide came back in, the pilot led us back out the way we had come in, and we waved goodbye to the little Pedregal panga at the surf line and headed out, none the worse for wear (except Flip, who claimed to have a funny metallic taste in his mouth, but we figured that was probably just his imagination).

We were *finally* ready for our epic whale quest and we headed out. We figured we'd make a big loop offshore off Costa Rica and back and hope that these blue whale rumors were true. We settled in to whale searching in earnest, eyes straining at the horizon.

The hours, and then days, wore on. Beebee and Amable became increasingly anxious the farther we got from shore, peering shoreward even when we were far out of the sight of land, and spending many a sleepless night as we shut down and drifted in the darkness. I'm not certain what they were on the lookout for, but Beebee's refrain every night was, "You go on to sleep now, me and Amable will be up all night, watchin'."

A sort of madness settled over us; we really wanted to find a blue whale. Only a quote from Melville's *Moby Dick* captures the mood:

"Towards thee I roll, thou all-destroying but unconquering whale; to the last I grapple with thee; from hell's heart I stab at thee; for hate's sake I spit my last breath at thee. Sink all coffins and all hearses to one common pool! and since neither can be mine, let me then tow to pieces, while still chasing thee, though tied to thee, thou damned whale!"

Well, we weren't quite there yet, but a certain craziness had definitely set in.

Hemlock Anyone?

One evening as we shut down after a particularly long, hot, and tedious day of scanning the empty horizon, Cherie decided to surprise us all with a treat and whipped up a fancy blended concoction; she had carefully scooped out the inside of our last watermelon, removed all of the seeds, added gin, and produced a pitcher of pink icy goodness she was just pouring out into large glasses when Beebee happened by. She handed him a glass. When she told him what was in it, he became apoplectic, immediately throwing the contents out over the side. Watermelon when mixed with alcohol became a deadly combination, he said, everyone knew that. What she was doing was equal to doling out pitcherfuls of poison in his view.

Now Cherie wanted to do the polite thing. She had no desire to upset anyone, but she was sure the drink was fine; she'd made lots of similar mixtures before. Besides, she'd worked hard on this and was proud of it. On top of that, we were getting low on both gin and watermelon, and she was damned if she would throw her creation out on the grounds of a silly superstition. So she declared she would take her chances and downed a big gulp. Some of the rest of us idled by about this time, and not realizing what was going on, availed ourselves of the mixture, and declaring it good, drank up.

Now Beebee and Amable were so upset by this development (or maybe just curious), that they put in a rare appearance that night down in the main cabin, watching us intently. It put everyone on edge, the whole deathwatch thing; it was a little awkward, and definitely put a crimp in the evening.

"More Jonestown Fizz, anyone?" Cherie asked brightly, with a sidelong glance at the watching gallery, when conversation flagged and our glasses ran low. She still makes that drink on occasion to this day and never fails to call it that.

Later that night, I awoke to a loud buzzing sound from the top deck—Beebee and Amable sacked out and snoring loudly, exhausted by the whole ordeal. At least they were finally getting some sleep.

Other Creatures of the Deep

The next day was when we spotted that weird beaked whale. It was like nothing I had ever seen before.

It was just one solitary animal, small dorsal fin, and a strange humped shape, brownish in color. It didn't stay around long, we just got a glimpse of it and it was gone, Flip didn't even have time to get in the water. Flip thought it might be something called a *Cuvier's* whale, but we couldn't be sure. That pitiful encounter was like the final straw. We were starting to get a little discouraged.

We started making our way back towards shore and began to see flocks of birds feeding here and there. Out of habit when I saw feeding birds I was reminded of the fishing lure Pancho had loaned me, and so in a moment of boredom I rigged it up and put it out, then pretty much forgot about it. Now I should have known better. If I had learned anything from all of those years of charter fishing, it is that if there is any magic on this planet it is contained in some fishing lures. You can have two plain resin plugs you swear are identical, and one will consistently produce fish and the other will never get touched, no rational explanation, just the way it is. This lure of Pancho's was obviously a magical lure, and I should have taken that into account.

We were idling along in calm seas, sleepily scanning the horizon as usual for flukes or blows, or anything, when suddenly the world exploded.

The reel was screaming as the line tore off it; behind the boat it looked like a bomb had gone off, white water flying everywhere. Rising from the center of the spray was the head and shoulders of the biggest blue marlin I had ever seen, probably a thousand pounds. Normally, a marlin will tail walk and dance along the surface when it first gets hooked, wearing itself out in the process, but this brute took one look at us and dove straight down, running out almost all of the line on the reel in a matter of moments and suddenly stopping, the

171

smoking reel showing just a few wraps left on the hub. The silence was deafening. We all just looked dumbly at the reel and each other for a second, and then everyone was urging somebody else to for God's sake grab the pole and start reeling. Everybody knew better than to take it. Reeling up a fish like that is bone-breaking, weary, hot work, especially if the animal dives immediately before expending lots of energy like this one had. Catching a fish like this could be a twelve or more hour process, and then what would we do with it if we got it to the boat? I hadn't thought this through when I put out that lure.

I put in a desultory hour gaining a few feet of line here and then giving it back there as the fish swam slowly along deep beneath us, a seesawing back and forth that I now was certain would last far into the night and maybe the next day, shades of *Old Man and the Sea*, so I made a decision. This wasn't what we were here for, and we weren't prepared to deal with it even if we caught it, so I tightened the drag and broke it off, knowing it would wear Pancho's lure like a pierced-lip kid at the mall for awhile, but it would live to fight another day. I saw Amable looking at me as I did it, and his eyes showed even more disdain than usual, if that was possible. This was possibly a record marlin, a lifetime opportunity in his eyes, and I had squandered it. And I felt terrible about Pancho's lure.

Out of the Comfort Zone

We reluctantly started heading back for the Panama border. The plan was to head back to Panamanian waters, clear back in to the country at the border town of Puerto Armuelles, and start making our way back to Panama City.

But we had no idea what had been happening while we had been at sea. Apparently things in Panama had been deteriorating. The first clue we had that there were some problems was when we routinely turned on the television on the boat as we were pulling up to the customs dock in Puerto Armuelles and were greeted by the image of General Noriega on the screen loudly berating the US in a televised address. Apparently the general was getting increasingly out of hand, and the US had just passed some sanctions against him.

The Panamanian border officials when they came aboard didn't exactly give us a warm and fuzzy feeling either. For one thing, only two of the group were in uniform, one was the customs guy, the other an armed Noriega Guardia Nacional officer, the other four or five seemed to be coming aboard just for the fun of it. They all seemed a little drunk.

They had us all line up with our paperwork in the main salon, and I didn't like the way they were looking at Cherie and Kathy. It was starting to look a little like that Humphrey Bogart scene in *Treasure of the Sierra Madre*. I wasn't about to ask any of them about any badges. I was regretting my part in getting everyone involved in this, especially the girls, this wasn't looking good.

But Beebee took the lead at this point. He took them aside, showed them the paperwork identifying the boat's owner, explained what we were doing, and handed over the bulk of the boat's liquor supply. This seemed to work wonders; we were all suddenly just a convivial group of people on a yacht. So we celebrated our new found friendship with a couple of drinks, bid our polite goodbyes, and we were free to be on our way.

Beebee had performed brilliantly, chatting and smiling with the officials, but, as we motored away, his uncharacteristic earnest expression showed me that even he had found the situation tense. I don't like to think how it could have turned out if the boat's owner hadn't been a buddy of the general's (a chance at the Miss Coiba title after all?) and I vowed, again, to be more careful in the future about escapades like this.

We took off on a beeline at this point back to home base in Panama City. Pancho was waiting for us on the dock. He had been trying to reach us, he said. Things were going to be a bit unsettled down here for a while. He and Marisa were leaving soon for their house in Miami, and he had arranged for us to fly out as soon as possible the next day. We hurriedly packed and said our goodbyes to Beebee and Amable, who seemed happy (and amazed) to be back, Amable even giving us a smile and hugs all around. They had done a good job and taken good care of us. It certainly wasn't their fault that we hadn't found our whales.

From our hotel room that night we got caught up on what had been happening from the television reports on CNN, and it was a weird experience. There had been an unsuccessful military coup against Noriega, and he had stepped up his repression tactics. There were even rumors that he might declare himself president and declare war on the US. It was definitely time to get out of there. We realized the televised riot scene we were watching was taking place right below us. But it was an odd thing: on television, it looked like the whole city was in an uproar, when we could see from our window that the demonstration was only about a block long.

It was scary, though, and even more so on our ride to the airport the next morning when our driver asked us to lie down out of sight. Demonstrators were throwing flaming pineapples over the streets, and our driver told us that they symbolized Noriega's head. The people called him *"Cara de Pina,"* or Pineapple Face, for his pockmarked complexion.

We were very glad to be flying home, but, as I was boarding the plane, I realized that in the excitement I had forgotten to tell Pancho about his lost lure. I knew he would be missing it. I guessed that would have to wait for gentler times.

The Blue Distance

We had an uneventful flight home, and we had just made it. Noriega did declare war on the US a short while later, and the US had responded immediately by invading the country and deposing him. It was a mess, and we could have been stuck in the middle of it. I heard later from Pancho and Marisa that they had made it safely to Miami in the nick of time (of course, this was Pancho we were talking about...I wasn't really worried). They said they'd be going back down in a few weeks after things settled back down.

Flip went on to get some great blue whale shots from various places in the world in the years to come, but never any from Central America, not yet anyway. There are still occasional reports of sightings down there, but so far no one has been back to check it out.

As for me, now when I spot a blue whale (there seem to be lots of them now in the Sea of Cortez), although I have a feeling of being fortunate to have a glimpse of this awesome creature, there is also a sense that they'd damned well better show themselves, after all we'd been through.

Two Weeks Before the Mast – Deliver Us

Escape from Paradise Island

It seems evident looking back on it just when an important change of direction in your life's path was taken (as Yogi Berra said: "*When you come to a fork in the road, take it...* "), but it isn't always all that obvious at the time that it happens. My getting involved with the small cruise ship business was one of those path-changing events, and it came about like this:

Although I was thoroughly enjoying my life in Maui, there did finally come a time when I was starting to experience what transplants to Hawaii often referred to as "rock fever"; that boxed-in feeling accompanied by an overwhelming need to get in a car and drive a few hundred miles without going in a circle, and without hearing pidgin (*Shaka brah...howzit?...*) spoken by every gas station attendant or fast food worker fresh off the plane and trying desperately to fit in.

So I took a break. Summer was winding down, and the winter fishing season in Lahaina hadn't started yet, so I took advantage of some idle time and flew back to the mainland to see some old friends and to visit with my parents, who had just moved from Oregon to

176

Washington. They had been telling me about this new place of theirs, and I was anxious to see it and them; I had been away for a few years.

When I got to Seattle I gave my folks a call. It turned out that their new house was on Whidbey Island, a beautiful island in Puget Sound a short ferry ride from Seattle, and my dad said he was anxious to show me something.

"You've gotta see what they are building down the road," he said, "you have to get in on this."

My father had always been an adventurous guy, an avid boater and pilot, and since he had retired he was constantly on the lookout for fun stuff to get his kids involved in, and I suspect it was so he could tag along and get in on it. I'd had him work aboard as a deckhand on Tad's boat when my folks came to visit me in Maui, and he'd never forgotten it.

The main employer on Whidbey was a shipbuilding company, Nichols Brothers Boat Builders, and he couldn't wait to take me over to their shipyard after I finally arrived at their place to show me the boat they were just getting ready to launch the next day. I hadn't been there an hour before he had me peering through the shipyard fence at what was poised to soon go down the ways into the water; it was one of the first little pocket cruise ships a company called Exploration Cruise Lines had just built. It was a great looking vessel, an actual miniature cruise ship. They had plans to build a fleet of these (this one was the second) to travel to exotic destinations like Alaska and Tahiti and Panama, and they had been advertising for help. I had to admit I was intrigued. The ship was bigger than anything I had ever worked on before, but I thought it wouldn't hurt to see what they were up to.

177

The christening party the next day was a big event; lots of flags and media and champagne bottles, the ship slipping gracefully off the ways into the water. I asked around to see if they were still hiring, more out of curiosity than anything else, since I assumed all of the hiring had already been done. I was directed to a tall, older guy standing at the edge of the crowd. It turned out to be Bob Giersdorf, recently of Alaska Airlines, and whose brainchild the new company was, and who I would eventually come to know well. But, at the time, I was just another kid asking about work. We chatted awhile, and he allowed that they were still looking for a few spots to fill in the crew, and he graciously gave me his card and invited me to come by the office the next day to meet the operations manager who was doing the hiring.

Incredible, there was still a chance. And the more I thought about this operation the more excited I got about the possibilities. After all, I had nothing tying me to Maui at the moment. I liked running the Sport Diver for Tad, but I knew there was a lineup of capable skippers who would leap at the job, and ditto for taking over the rent on my Lahaina apartment, not to mention inheriting my Maui Cruiser car, roaches and all. But it was a big decision. I had fallen into such an idyllic life in paradise that it seemed almost criminal to leave it. But this new opportunity exerted a real exotic pull. Alaska, Panama, Tahiti, all places I had never been. I lay awake all night thinking. I finally decided I had nothing to lose by at least going to the interview. And besides, there was no guarantee they would hire me anyway. So the next morning I borrowed one of my dad's ties, wrestled my unkempt self into some degree of kemptness, and made my way to the interview.

178

The operations manager was an old Alaska hand named Chuck Kearns, whom I would also come to know well, and we hit it off immediately. We had a great visit, talking about boats and nautical tales and life in general. They had already hired a captain for this boat, he told me (an ex-Navy guy he said), but there was still a first mate spot available, and if my license had an ocean endorsement (which being from Hawaii it did), then I might be considered for the spot. But I had to decide soon because they were heading to Panama in a couple of weeks.

There was no way I could pass up an opportunity like this. I called Chuck the next day, told him I was interested, and I was in. I would simply need to come by the office to process paperwork, get some shots for traveling to the tropics, get fitted for uniforms, and come aboard. I called Maui and told Tad and everyone the exciting news. My life was off in a new direction.

Now it must be said I had no idea how to operate a ship of that size, even though my license qualified me for it. I had spent almost my whole career on sport fishing boats. I hadn't even used radar, which was important in this job. But I assumed they knew my background, it was in my application material, so I figured I would be trained accordingly. And besides, I'd never let a little thing like no prior experience stop me from trying things before. But this was a little different; in this case I would be responsible for more than just myself.

Reporting for Doody

I showed up at the ship the next day, bright-eyed and eager, excited about this new adventure and ready to begin. I was anxious to meet the captain. Being the only other watch officer on board meant he and I would be working closely together. I knew I had a lot to learn. I was picturing my mentor as a wise and kindly old salt, a patient mariner, a Spencer Tracy look-alike with a cap and a pipe and a twinkle in his eye.

The ship was abuzz with activity, the crew, young college-age kids for the most part, were bringing equipment and stores aboard and lashing down gear, lots of yelling and laughter echoing from everywhere. I hailed a girl in mid-flight rushing by carrying a pile of linens to ask her where I might find the captain. She stopped short and regarded me with a frank appraising look when she saw I was wearing a uniform shirt and carrying a crew handbook.

"If you are looking for Captain Wrangler I'd try his throne up on the bridge, but I'd tuck in that shirt first if I were you," she informed me as she hurried off.

Huh. I had put on one of the new crew polo shirts I had been given, thinking it would be a nice touch for my first day, and as I looked around I noticed that everyone was wearing a similar shirt, and they were all tucked into matching uniform pants as well, the overall result was that they looked much spiffier than I did. The rest of the crew had all been going through company indoctrination and training classes for a couple of weeks prior to joining the ship, but since I had been hired so late, I had missed that step, so I was going to be a bit behind on some of the procedural issues, but I was sure I'd get caught up. I did tuck my shirt into my jeans (I had almost worn the usual shorts and flip flops I was used to wearing in Hawaii, but luckily had thought better of it at the last minute) and had a quick look around.

What an incredible boat. To me, it seemed huge. A big galley and crew area were aft, with walk-in freezers and engineering spaces below. The lower and middle decks held staterooms and dining and lounge areas, the upper deck also had staterooms and a large covered open area containing deck furniture and the large inflatable shore boats that were to be used to shuttle passengers ashore. I couldn't wait to check it all out more thoroughly. But, for now, I thought I'd better check in with the boss.

I climbed several sets of stairs up to the uppermost deck and made my way forward to the pilothouse. When I opened the door, there, as reported, sat Captain Wrangler.

I'm a little Despot, Short and Stout...

I have to say my first impression was not positive. My first view of my new shipmate was of a little scowling man in full captain's uniform, shoulder boards and all, lounging in the big captain's bridge chair, legs crossed and sucking on a toothpick. The toothpick in the side of his mouth turned out to be a regular affectation, notwithstanding any proximity to meal times and, for some reason, became a future source of constant irritation to me. His little beady eyes fixed on me, checking me out from head to toe; the rest of him didn't move.

He didn't say a word, just scowled. He was waiting for me to speak; initiating conversation was beneath him it seemed. Or maybe that toothpick was engaging too much of his attention. Whatever, this didn't look good. Maybe there was a reason the mate position hadn't been filled yet.

I barged ahead and stuck out my hand. "Captain Wrangler? I'm Captain Bennett, your new first mate." He regarded my outstretched hand as if it was some distasteful animal, a naked mole rat with string warts perhaps, and he made no move to take it.

He slowly reached up and removed the toothpick, then spoke. "You're out of uniform," he said.

I wasn't used to the whole military chain-of-command business. My first response was along the surely-you-must-be-joking line, but that wasn't the case; incredibly, this little guy was serious. It was clear that if I wanted to continue on this adventure I'd have to play along, so I decided that is what I would do.

"Sorry," I said, pulling back my hand (I couldn't quite bring myself to add *sir*, it was just too foreign to me) and explained my newcomer status. He explained that he ran a tight Navy ship and that his crew would be in uniform at all times. I didn't have a problem with that; this was going to be interesting. In fact, I decided I was looking forward to it. I didn't have to like this guy; I just had to figure out how to work with him.

He didn't strike me as what I thought an ex-Navy captain should be like, however. But he handed me a card that read *"Captain Wrangler, USN (retired),"* so there it was. Later I found out that even though he was indeed retired from the Navy, he had actually retired as a Boson's mate, not a Captain. He had gotten his Coast Guard captain's license later, the same way I had, so the card he'd had printed was a little misleading. It went a long way toward explaining his command style, however. I learned volumes from him, mainly how not to treat the crew when I became a captain.

For the moment there was a lot to do, however. As first mate, I was put in charge of the deck crew. The ship personnel were divided into two main groups, the deck crew consisted of the deckhands, engineers and the like, and then there was the hotel staff, the stewards, cooks, bartenders, etc., who were overseen by the hotel manager. There was also a purser, who acted as the liaison among everybody. It seemed like a complex arrangement, but it actually made sense and was apparently the way ships had been organized for years.

We were going to be leaving in about a week for our trip to Panama, going down with just a skeleton crew, with the rest of the staff flying down to meet us when we got there. We were taking on last minute supplies, things we thought it might be difficult to get down there, like paint and spare engine parts, and stowing and lashing everything that might come loose in the inevitable rough weather we knew we would encounter on the trip. I was getting caught up in the excitement of the whole thing; we were mostly just a bunch of kids making it up as we went along.

As departure time approached, those of us going on the trip went on a shopping spree to stock up on our favorite foods to last us the two weeks or so it would take us to get to Panama. Steaks and chickens and hams were favorites, spareribs and prime ribs galore filled the big walk-in freezer and refrigerator. The company had said to spare no expense for whatever food we wanted to bring, and we took them up on it. None of us could believe this one deckhand, though, a guy named Griff; all he stocked up on were cases of canned Spaghetti-O's. It was his favorite food and all that he wanted, no one could talk him into anything else. Oh well, to each his own we figured. Poor guy, we all wondered what kind of childhood trauma had led to *that* fixation, but we were all too busy planning our own upcoming feasts to give it much thought.

Shortly before we departed, Captain Wrangler gathered all of us going on the trip together and assigned us our watch standing duties. He said he would be taking the daylight hours on the bridge, and the night duty he assigned to me and a deckhand we all called Big Red. It was a bit unusual. Normally, watch standing duties are spread out over different times of the day, with a certain number of hours on and off duty, which ends up dividing daylight and night watches equally, but that wasn't the way this captain wanted to do it. I couldn't blame him; night watches can be stressful, especially in rough weather when you can't see the waves coming, and especially when they last all night every night. But we didn't know any better at the time. We were just anxious to get started.

And then it headed south...

I had been studying my radar plotting and operation training material. Our first few nights on watch were in dense fog and heavy ship traffic, so the radar was becoming our best friend. It was like playing a high stakes video game when you knew you only had one man and no replay. It didn't take long to get the knack of it, though, so I didn't have to embarrass myself by calling for help; all of my training was coming back to me.

Big Red turned out to be great company. He was a big lanky redheaded country boy fresh off the farm going to sea for adventure, so everything was new to him. He had a great sense of humor and knew lots of stories, so the first few nights passed quickly without incident.

The weather turned rough about the third night out, however, and it really didn't let up the rest of the way to Central America. Not good news. This was when Big Red and I both discovered we were prone to seasickness.

Now seasickness, to those who have never experienced it, there is no way to describe it. And to those who have, there is no need to describe it. Pure misery. Chart plotting becomes a focused hell, and radar plotting even worse. Anything that requires the victim to concentrate on anything other than brute survival is excruciatingly miserable. Big Red and I both had our respective garbage cans in which to vomit at regular intervals, and the night watches dragged on interminably. Captain Wrangler wanted a recorded chart plot at thirty minute intervals and we started recording our miserable way down the coast.

The next night was so rough it was all we could do to hang on, the ship pounding and lurching. Big Red was tossed up and onto the chart table when we crashed into a particularly huge wave, scattering charts and navigation equipment everywhere. I got things straightened back up and set about making another plot when I saw a small smeared mark near our position Red had somehow made on his way across the chart.

"Red, what the hell is this you left on the chart?" I asked him. His head was deep into his garbage can at this point, so his voice sounded like he was talking from the bottom of a well when he replied.

"Big Red's Dick Print," he responded miserably. Who knew what it really was. I didn't press him on it. He was in no mood to chat. He sounded downright testy, actually.

So I circled the mark, labeled it BRDP, and put the time next to it.

The next morning, Captain Wrangler put in his usual surly appearance, after the sun had come up and things were more civilized, and I gave him the usual briefing, noting that BRDP had taken place at 0235. He just nodded with his usual scowl, and I knew right then that he would never ask me what BRDP stood for, fearing that there might be some navigational procedure that I knew about and he didn't. I could just picture him frantically searching through reference books later, toothpick bouncing up and down, looking for BRDP, Bearing Range Deviation Point or something, what...? From that night forward, we never failed to plot a spurious BRDP, putting it down at different times, and dutifully reporting it in the morning briefing, and he always acknowledged it with a grunt. He never asked what it stood for, I knew he wouldn't. Years later, I saw those same charts we used on that trip, with BRDPs still faithfully plotted all the way down the coast; no one had erased them. I guess they didn't know what they were.

Nutty Deviation

Things calmed down a bit after we got into Mexican waters, and the long misery of our night watches abated somewhat. It seemed there was always some minor crisis or another happening though, some little fishing boat without lights in our path, or a flock of birds cluttering up the radar and looking like an oncoming island. One night, we seemed to be set by a powerful current or something throwing us off course. We had to steer over twenty degrees to the left of the course we were trying to make; it seemed weird. It was bothering me; I couldn't figure it out.

I started to plot our position again, taking up the pointed dividers to measure our distance from the coast, when an unexpected wave rolled us enough to make me lose my balance and stumble. Then, all hell broke loose. Big Red suddenly started screaming and rolled out of the helm chair onto the deck, yelling and thrashing around. I couldn't tell what was happening in the dark. The ship's auto pilot suddenly swung the ship hard right, and I was lurching around trying to get us straightened out and trying to figure out what could have happened to Red.

He was moaning and cursing and wouldn't answer my shouts. I finally found the bridge light switch, and, in the sudden glare, I could see Red curled up in the corner rocking back and forth holding his bare foot, blood dripping between his fingers, the can of peanuts he had been snacking from by the helm chair knocked onto the deck with spilled peanuts everywhere. It took awhile before we could sort out what had happened.

It seemed that when I had gotten knocked off balance, I had plunged the needle-sharp points of the dividers into Red's big toe; he had been sitting in the helm chair in the dark with his bare feet up on the console by the metal can of peanuts he was eating from, which he had placed next to the compass. He had no idea what had happened to his foot in the dark. All he knew was that something horrible had bitten him. The magnetic metal peanut can had been what was throwing the autopilot off course, and he had involuntarily kicked it out of the way when the metal spikes on the dividers hit him, so the ship had corrected suddenly; all in all it had been quite exciting. We didn't feel it was necessary to include that drama in our morning briefing, and I don't think I ever did see Red eat another peanut. That episode made him jumpy whenever he saw me reach for the dividers after that. He may have thought I'd done it on purpose.

The Big Thaw

Things were actually starting to go along well. We had established our routines and all was rolling along on schedule. It couldn't last of course. We were somewhere down off Guatemala when the refrigeration gave out. The engineers said there was nothing to be done until we reached port, so we were in a bit of a pickle. We had of course been counting on refrigeration when we had

187

bought all of that fancy food back in Seattle, almost everything we had was frozen, and it was thawing out fast in the tropical heat. We had a couple of days of gorging on our favorite things, and then we had to start throwing stuff over the side. It was heartbreaking. Steaks and roasts and turkeys, prime ribs and racks of lamb, of course the milk and produce, no more ice cream for the likes of us. Things started to turn funny colors. It is a sobering thing to pry a purple chicken out of the hands of a weeping deckhand and toss it in the ocean, but it had to be done.

We were still a couple of days out from Panama, so we had some hard decisions to make. Then all eyes turned to Griff's stash of canned Spaghetti-O's. They were quickly appropriated (over Griff's plaintive protests), and a rationing system was initiated. The needs of the many easily trumped Griff's pitiful objections; this was survival. After all, we told him, this way we wouldn't have to draw straws to see who would be eaten first; it could well have turned out to be him. Everybody got a can per day from what was left of his prodigious supply, which would keep us from starving until we got to civilization, along with the cookies and chips and other accouterments we'd brought.

Pilot Lit

Finally, the lights of Panama City came into view one night around midnight. We had called ahead to arrange for a harbor pilot to bring us in to the dock, and he was scheduled to come aboard at two o'clock that morning. We spent an hour or so drifting around in the designated pilot zone waiting, when finally we saw the little pilot launch making its way out to us from the entrance to the canal. We got the launch secured at the stern, and then helped aboard one of the most inebriated human beings I have ever encountered in my life; our designated harbor pilot as it turned out.

I was impressed. This guy was incredibly bombed, but he was still getting around and talking a mile a minute. He was one of those loquacious drunks who emote continuously in a booming voice, accompanied by dramatic hand gestures, and he was in fine form. We were all awake at that point, and we helped him up to the bridge. He was putting on quite a performance, shouting orders and shaking hands all around. He reeled into the pilothouse, steadied himself against the chart table with both hands, and began giving orders.

"Half-ahead, steady up on 350 degrees, let's take her in boys...whup...watch that buoy there...all ahead full, time's a-wastin'...." He seemed to be in a hurry, we had apparently interrupted him in the midst of some celebration or other.

We started making our way in to the canal entrance, all seemed in order. We could see the dock we were headed for off to the right of the canal itself, it was designated on our chart. All we had to do was get there and tie up. But then the pilot suddenly severely startled us all by starting to yell and point.

"Outbound ship, outbound ship!" he screamed, and backed up a couple of steps and promptly fell down into the stairwell behind him in the dark. Now we were all straining our eyes ahead to see into the darkness, but there was nothing there, not visually and not on radar. There were some lights on shore that lined up to look like a ship's running lights, that must have been what he was reacting to, but there was certainly no outbound ship. This was getting ridiculous; fun as this guy was, all we wanted to do was get tied up and off this thing for a

189

while. We elected to just keep going, while the pilot thrashed around at the bottom of the stairway, apparently having some trouble getting himself back upright and ambulatory, and we didn't feel any need at that point to hurry him along.

By the time he got himself straightened out and made his way back up to the bridge, we were almost to the dock, and he began lurching around and yelling unintelligible things at the line handlers waiting to take our lines, all memory of the alleged outbound ship apparently forgotten. We got tied up without incident, got the gangway down, and helped our friendly pilot off to return to whatever festivities we had interrupted. As he stumbled away, everybody shared a wide-eyed look. We'd finally made it. But what kind of place had we made it to?

Bungle in the Jungle

The next morning seemed almost surreal after the long days and nights of our routine at sea. The process of having to regain land legs after a long sea voyage turns out to be absolutely true; all of us were staggering around on the dock like Deadheads at a free concert, the ground mysteriously heaving and shifting under our feet.

Meanwhile, the rest of our crew had arrived from the airport fresh and ready to get the ship back in shape for our first trip, along with a number of new Panamanian crew who had been hired down there. The cruise line was thinking that incorporating some local people into the crew mix would not only add a local cultural flavor to the experience, but also their local knowledge could prove invaluable in getting the operation side up and going, and it turned out they were right on both counts.

It was a flurry of activity, and it was coming together, but there was still one more important thing we had to accomplish before we could start on our first trip with passengers.

The company had advertised that we would be traveling up the Mogue River in the Darien Jungle to visit with a primitive tribe of Choco Indians they had located there, which was all well and good, but nobody had charted out the river route to the village yet, and our first trip was only a couple of weeks away. Somebody needed to charter a small boat to see if we could even get up there by water. That somebody turned out to be me. Captain Wrangler had his hands full getting the ship back in shape and browbeating the new crew, so I was the logical choice. I wasn't looking forward to getting back out on the water just days after finally getting to dry land, but it had to be done. It turned out to be quite an adventure in itself and how I met the legendary Pancho.

We chartered a fishing boat from one of the Panama Canal Ship Pilots, (a different, but no more temperate bunch than the Harbor Pilots), a guy named Jerry, who had grown up in the Canal Zone and knew his way around the waters. Jerry said he would fuel and provision his boat and pick me up at the Balboa Dock the following night.

I was waiting at the dock the next night at the appointed time, and sure enough, out of the darkness came Jerry with his little sportfishing boat, the *Roncador*. It looked perfect. I hopped aboard with my bag and we were off. Jerry's plan was to make it as far as the island of Contadora to anchor that first night, and then push on down to the Darien Jungle the next day.

There turned out to be a couple of other people aboard, a Panamanian deckhand named Carlos, who

Jerry said also knew some of the Choco dialect (they didn't speak Spanish, and we needed help with our communications), and a big blond very drunk guy who introduced himself as Pancho, who it seemed had no reason to be along but for the adventure. Typical Pancho it turned out.

We set out into the darkness, and I started to get to know my shipmates. Jerry and I were sitting up on the bridge chatting and watching the lighthouse on Contadora get closer, when Pancho made his way out on to the transom for a tipsy bathroom break, and Jerry told me to keep a close eye on him. He said that not only was he the vice president and son of the owner of the ship agency we were using, he was also a vice-consul at the US embassy, and there would be hell to pay if he fell overboard and drowned on our watch; he was a Very Important Person down here, and it was our responsibility to watch out for him. No kidding. I was starting to get the impression that things were done a little differently in Panama.

Up the Creek

This little excursion turned out to be one of the most fun boat trips I've ever had. Pancho (his real name was Frank) turned out to be great company, a real character, and we've shared many adventures and been friends ever since. We all had a ball, fishing on the way down the coast, and then making our way to the mouth of the Mogue River, where we anchored to await high tide to do our exploration. Jerry maneuvered the *Roncador* deep into the jungle when the tide was right, sloths and parrots occasionally appearing in the branches overhead, taking depth soundings and charting as we went.

We eventually made contact with the primitive, nearly naked and blue-painted Chocos at their village.

The scene was right out of *National Geographic*; a cluster of reed huts along the river, with topless women squatting around cooking fires, naked kids running around everywhere. We met with the chief, an amused-looking wizened little guy with a loincloth, a Moe of Three Stooges haircut, and blue lines drawn all over his face and body. Carlos was chatting away with him in what we all assumed was Choco (I think Carlos assumed it was, too), ostensibly setting up the times we would be coming to visit them. The little guy was nodding away and smiling, and we were feeling good about our arrangements. It turned out they had no idea who we were or what we wanted, however, as we found out later. They hadn't understood a word. Apparently, Carlos' professed grasp of the Choco dialect wasn't all that he had hoped or claimed. The Chocos assumed we were from the Panamanian Health Services, the only other white people they had had any dealings with, which caused no end of confusion when we showed up with a hundred or so passengers later who just wanted to wander around their village and look at them, but those are stories for another time. For now, we were feeling smug at the way we had pulled all of this off. We headed off downriver secure in the satisfaction of a job well done.

Let the Show Begin

Things were in an uproar when I got back to the ship. Chuck was there, along with several other people from the head office, and a couple of new mates. It seemed that the captain of the company's other ship, the one currently in Tahiti, had experienced some family emergency and would need to fly home. They wanted Captain Wrangler to head there immediately to take over that operation and wanted to offer me the position of

193

relief captain of this one, with the help of the two new mates they had brought down with them. I couldn't believe it. Just a few weeks ago, I was hoping to get on the ship in any capacity, was ecstatic about getting hired as a mate, and now they were offering me the captain's position. Of course I would do it. It was like being in one of those dreams you recognize as only a dream, so you can just sit back and watch it unfold. It had a surreal quality to it, but I was confident I could do it, not knowing then what I didn't know then, as they say.

We sat down for a meeting in the ship's office, and I got an introduction to my new mates. The new first mate was an intense short-statured guy (with the unfortunate last name of Little), who had just come off a job running dynamite ships to some mining operations up in Alaska (which could have explained some of the outrageous religious views he exhibited later). The other guy, the new second mate, was an old tugboat hand named Tugboat Dewey (*"just call me Tugboat"*), who had lots of experience running tugs and barges in the canal and the locks, but whose emotional maturity came into question immediately.

One of the things we were soon to learn about Tugboat was his consistency; he was what he was (as Popeye said) namely a big kid, and he never tried to pretend otherwise. He had been working away at some wire and rubber band contraption the whole time we were talking as we made our way to the office, and, as the meeting began, it became evident what it was: a crude homemade fart machine. It was a wound up paddle arrangement that he slipped beneath himself as he sat down and unleashed at intervals by leaning sideways, and since he had sat himself on top of a metal file cabinet, it made quite a racket. No one could believe it.

194

Here we were, just meeting each other for the first time, discussing some serious matters, and here was this guy ratcheting off fart noises and struggling to keep a straight face. It was incredible. I loved it. This was going to be fun, and I couldn't wait to see how it turned out. I could never have imagined only a few short weeks ago that I would end up here in this position at this moment. The passengers were due to arrive in a couple of days, and I guessed we were as ready as we would ever be.

Isthmus Holidays

Jungle All the Way…

With a couple of Exploration Cruise Lines Panama trips under our belt, the ship's crew was starting to settle into a routine. The newness and nerves of our first couple of trips with passengers was starting to wear off, and, in truth, we were all more than a little proud of the way everything had gone. The passengers had loved the experiences, and, despite a few minor surprises (like the Choco Indians having no idea who we were when we first showed up at their village), everything had gone splendidly. The food, the crew, the schedule, the activities and stops had all been extraordinary. We were all feeling pretty good, like maybe we could actually pull this off. Then came that Christmas trip.

We were beginning to understand that each group of passengers, even though they were made up of many different elements from many different places, all had their own distinct personalities. But we weren't prepared for the group that came aboard in Cristobel over Christmas that December. I can't blame it entirely on the passengers, though; in retrospect, the crew did some unraveling of their own. I suspect maybe it had something to do with the time of year, but I can't be sure. In the case of the passengers, you have to be a little suspicious of people who knowingly schedule trips to be away from home and relatives over the holidays, there must be some underlying reason they want to put some distance between themselves and hearth and kin during that time. As for the crew, some were probably a little homesick, not being used to being so far from home during this season. But, for whatever reasons, things came undone on this trip. It started with a train wreck, naturally enough.

The Wrong Foot

We would routinely alternate the departure port of the trip between Balboa (on the Pacific side), and Cristobel (on the Atlantic). That way, we would only have to do a single transit of the canal per trip, since it was a fairly expensive and time-consuming operation. This particular trip was scheduled to start on the Cristobel side, which normally required the passengers to be transferred from the airport to the little antique passenger train that ran along the canal between Balboa and Cristobel to travel to the ship, which usually made for a quaint and scenic first leg of their adventure. But shortly before the passengers were to board the train, word came that the thing had derailed earlier somewhere around Gatun Lake, and service would be suspended indefinitely. This caused no end of stress and confusion as luggage and passengers were gathered up and put on hastily chartered buses. And of course the usual complimentary open bar that resulted from any little unforeseen inconvenience like this awaited the guests when they arrived at the ship, and this group tucked into it with unusual gusto. That may have set the tone right there. I'm not sure a certain percentage of them drew a completely sober breath for the entire remainder of the week.

The Welcome Aboard Captain's Dinner that night was a first indication of how things would go. It was late because of the train snafu, and we were still at the dock waiting for some misplaced luggage when dinner started. Then, a large portion of the passengers were drunk from that complimentary open bar. And there was the whole holiday spirit thing on top of everything else. It seemed we started off balance and never recovered.

Bird Sightings

Our first sign of trouble came when it seemed two different groups had inadvertently been promised a seat that night at the captain's table; one a prestigious group of ornithologists, bird-watchers gathering material for a book about the birds of Central America, and the other the officer elite of a quasi-official boating regulation organization known as the *Power Squadron*, a mostly ex-military bunch who traveled together as a group on trips like this, and fancied themselves master mariners. The bird watchers won out on this competition by virtue of arriving at the table first, probably because they weren't as handicapped by early alcohol consumption, but the *Power Squadron* group was clearly unhappy at the supposed slight, especially, it seemed, the wives. They were only slightly mollified by the solemn promise that they could watch me eat on a subsequent night. Normally, the honor of joining the captain for dinner was won at a bingo game or some such thing, but, for them, an exception would be arranged. I couldn't wait.

The bird watching group was charming company at dinner, and it struck me how the individuals each resembled different aspects of a bird in some way. A sharp beaked face there, colorful plumage there. I continued pouring champagne and chatting amiably with the feathered women on either side of me, hoping for the best.

Then, midway through the meal, I saw it. There underneath the mashed potatoes on my plate was, incredibly, a picture of a woman's naked breast! A pair of them actually, I discovered as I moved potatoes aside. I looked under the asparagus, and more graphic female anatomy revealed itself. I froze. I don't know how long I sat staring at my plate; time seemed to stand still. I finally came to my senses and covered up the lewd display, just in the nick of time as my dinner companions suddenly all swung their eyes my way in response to some unheard question one of them had asked me.

"Sorry?" I stammered, smoothing mashed potatoes over as much of my plate as possible. Someone had cut up a Playboy centerfold and taped it to my plate before putting food over it. I glanced toward the galley, and there peeking between the slats of the shade over the serving window were the mirthful eyes of the suspected perpetrators, evil chefs Robin and Cherie, laughing uncontrollably, obviously much amused. What the hell was going on around here? It was like the whole ship was on catnip.

Dessert appeared, something called Banana Foster, which involved a spectacular flaming presentation; but on this night, it may have been too liberally doused with rum. The resulting fireball was especially spectacular, but it did some damage to the waiter's hair and eyebrows before the conflagration was doused. I swear the poor server, a young kid named Houston, was still smoking as he served us our portions, the smell of burned hair compromising the experience somewhat, and his singed eyebrows giving the distinct impression of a pair of electrocuted caterpillars crawling across his forehead. Things were sliding out of control, and we hadn't even left the dock yet.

Incoming

We made it through dinner, the missing luggage appeared, and we were finally able to get underway. I turned the watch over to Captain Little, who was running as first mate, and made my way to my stateroom, already worn out. The weather report didn't sound good for later in the evening, so I thought I'd try to get a little sleep before my midnight watch.

I was sharing the captain's stateroom just behind the pilothouse with second mate Tugboat Dewey for this trip, since we had a full complement of passengers and every available stateroom was taken. Tugboat was sleeping on the bottom bunk when I got there, so I quietly made my way into my top bunk and settled in.

Now I should explain a little about my two mates. They were both competent mariners, but each had their own idiosyncrasies, to put it mildly. They were about as opposite as could be, and this had lead to some misunderstandings between them. Tugboat was just a big kid full of practical jokes and coarse good humor; nothing seemed to faze him. Captain Little on the other hand had just come from running a dynamite ship for the mining industry up in Alaska, and was wound up a bit tight. He was also a devout follower of some sort of fundamentalist religious sect, which may or may not have had anything to do with his previous dynamite job, but that was okay with me as long as it didn't affect his work. The only evident symptom of his enlightened state was a tendency to quietly pray over some of the most inconsequential things imaginable, as if his Supreme Being would have an interest in fixing a broken windshield wiper, for example.

I was almost asleep when I heard something that didn't sound right. On those ships, it was possible to hear from the captain's stateroom what was going on in the pilothouse through the bulkhead when everything was quiet, and I heard the marine radio being turned up very loud, and Captain Little quietly praying for some guidance. Apparently, there had been some radio announcements from some inbound ship heading for the canal entrance, but no evidence of the ship on radar, and since the entrance was relatively narrow Captain Little was getting a little worked up trying to determine its location. And then I heard it again:

"This is the *Gigantus Maru*, inbound at..." and then just staticky noise. It was strange; it also seemed to be coming from inside our room, from down below me. And the staticky noise sounded suspiciously like someone clearing their throat. It was Tugboat from under his pillow, screwing with Little with a low-powered handheld radio.

"Tugboat, knock it off!" I said. "Sorry, Captain, thought you were asleep," he responded, then silence. I was too tired to bawl him out for that kind of behavior again; I'd get to that later. What a horrible little kid he must have been. In fact, he had told us some stories about when he was growing up that illustrated just how horrible. He'd related how he'd had a hobby of making flying model rockets and had developed an experimental program of sending "cryogenically suspended frogs" (frogs put into hibernation by freezing them into ice cubes), up in the nose cones of his rockets to be parachuted back to earth. That is until his nearsighted mom had distributed those frog-laden ice cubes into drinks at a cocktail party and they woke up; it sounded like it had turned into quite a lively gathering. I wondered if it was too late to get him on to a Ritalin drug program; that's what I would have done if he'd been my kid...maybe I still could. At least there were no more radio calls from the *Gigantus Maru* for the moment.

San Blasted

When I woke up for my midnight watch, the weather had indeed deteriorated, just as advertised. This leg from Cristobel to the San Blas Islands was usually the roughest part of the whole trip, which was the down side of starting from this side of the canal; the first night was usually a bit uncomfortable. Going the other way, passengers had a chance to get used to being aboard ship gradually; the weather was usually calmer on the Pacific side. We always warned everyone, and liberally distributed seasick pills, when heading out from the Atlantic side. But this night was turning out to be a little rockier than usual.

I made a quick tour of the ship before heading to the bridge. All looked in good shape until I got to the staterooms on the second deck, where I saw this old man, naked and on all fours, halfway out of his room, with the sliding door to his stateroom sliding back and forth into his middle with each roll of the ship. He was one of those shrunken bald guys who always remind me of a turtle, in this case a seasick turtle. A deckhand also making rounds showed up at this point. Together, we got the guy back in bed and lashed down, and made his wife promise to keep him there.

When I made my way up to the bridge, there sat Captain Little in the helm chair, arms crossed and pivoting 180 degrees back and forth with each roll of the ship.

"*Well...*" he said, pivoting forward, "I wonder how they are liking the *informality...*" pivoting back, "of a *small* cruise vessel experience..." pivoting forward, " *now?*" quoting from a selling point in the brochure.

I had neither the time nor inclination to discuss it with him at the moment. I got up to speed on our position and status and relieved him of the watch. We only had a few more hours of this to go until we got into calmer waters, and then it would be smooth sailing for the rest of the trip, so all was good.

We pulled into the lee of the San Blas Island area just about sunrise, and it was a calm and beautiful morning. These islands are some of the most perfect and lovely little islands in the world, white sandy beaches and palm trees, some of the tiniest of the 300 or so islands have only a single coconut palm surrounded by white sand, exactly the kind of cartoon island you see where the guy gets shipwrecked alone with the beautiful woman, that kind of thing.

We dropped anchor to just relax and rest for awhile after our crossing, and I headed down to get an early breakfast, feeling all was right with the world. Just as I started down the companionway, I met a guy coming up who was wearing the most extraordinary pair of pants. They were bright green and covered with tiny blue spouting whales. I'd never seen anything like it; I couldn't take my eyes off them, where would you wear something like that? A high-stakes miniature golf tournament? I couldn't help myself, I blurted out, "WOW! Now *that* is a pair of PANTS!"

As my eyes traveled up to his face on the way by, instead of the self-deprecating jokester kind of guy I expected to be wearing something like that, I met the hostile stare of a very uptight citizen; it was an icy moment as we passed.

A short time after I went below, the purser cornered me with a wide-eyed look. Apparently, there was a passenger and his wife who wanted to speak with the captain immediately. After that rough night they wanted off this ship. They didn't care how, but they were adamant: they wanted off.

Uh oh. I had a bad feeling as I went to the ship's office for the meeting. Sure enough, the first thing I saw upon entering was a green pair of pants. We shared an awkward moment. They hadn't slept a wink, they said, and they wanted a helicopter to come and pick them up, they didn't care what it cost. I had the impression they were used to getting their way.

It took a lot of persuading, promising that the worst was over, extolling the wonders of the upcoming trip, that kind of thing, but we finally convinced them to stay aboard. It was quite a performance. Inspired. I think unconsciously I just didn't want to lose the chance to buy those pants.

I was worn out again; the fun just never seemed to end.

After breakfast we pulled anchor and started to head over to our first stop, a little island called Wichub Walla, home to some of the Kuna Indians whom we had come to visit. Shortly after we got under way, a remarkable little man came uninvited into the bridge. He was a compact little guy with a crew-cut and Bermuda shorts, a Marine Corps tattoo, and a big unlit cigar sticking out of his mouth. He took up a position next to the helm with his hands on his hips and announced that he was an Admiral in the *Power Squadron*, and then, incredibly, farted. We were all speechless. What?

I wasn't sure how to react. We were all proud of our open-bridge policy; it seemed like a nice gesture and an important part of the trip to allow people to visit the bridge when conditions were good, but this was going to be a bit trying. Apparently, he thought his announcement was sufficiently awe-inspiring that there was no need for any follow-up; he waited in silence for us to respond. Somebody asked him politely where he was from, for lack of anything else to say, and it turned out he was from Oklahoma City. We confessed that we hadn't realized that there was sufficient water around Oklahoma City to require the existence of a branch of the *Power Squadron* there, but it turned out that oh yes there were lots of boats on the lakes, and lots of boaters in need of guidance. He was obviously going to keep an eye on us. He was to become, I feared, a regular visitor.

We had our hands full at the moment, however, wending our way through the chain of islands, almost every island inhabited by the colorful mola-wearing Kunas, with their little sailing dugouts swarming around the channels. The Kunas were a wiry, industrious, tough, and unique race. There were thousands of them living around here, and they lived by their own rules. First the Spanish, then the English and then the Panamanians had tried to conquer them, but everybody who tried had gotten their butts kicked. They were like Island Apaches. The last time Panama had tried to enforce sovereignty, they had hung the invaders from poles and lit them on fire, so now everybody pretty much left them alone. They had become very adept traders, however, and what we had come to trade for mostly were the beautifully crafted reverse appliqué mola panels the women made for their apparel. But you haven't been in shopping combat until you've gotten into a bargaining war with a crafty, pipe-smoking Kuna grandmother. Tough negotiators. We warned everybody not to try to take their picture without paying them first; I didn't want to see any of our passengers lit on fire.

Beach Invasion

The ships back then were set up for a nifty technique called bow landing. Basically, we would just ease the ship ashore and extend a big gangway straight off the bow to the beach, a great feature that worked perfectly in a place like San Blas that didn't have docks. It shook the Kunas up the first time we did it, though. As we got closer and closer to the beach they were yelling and waving us away, and as we pulled onto the sand, they scattered and ran. They had so much fun that first time that they now reenacted the whole scenario every time we showed up.

This time was no exception. A big, colorful crowd was gathered on the beach in Wichub Walla, women in colorful head scarves and molas, many with parakeets perched on their heads and the ever-present pipes, yelling and waving, then scattering and running at the last second as the bow loomed over them and the gangway came down. It was much like the alien spaceship landing in the movie *The Day the Earth Stood Still*, except we were carrying a lot of little monsters instead of one big one.

We disgorged our hundred or so passengers onto the island: blue haired ladies in sun hats swarming over the mola displays, determined to find the best molas and part with their money, our excitable Panamanian expedition leader Antonio talking a mile a minute and

206

leading the way. It was always quite a sight, like someone kicking over a termite mound.

We would spend that first day island hopping, and doing beach barbeque and snorkel stops all through the San Blas area, a magical place. The Kunas liked to have all visitors out of their territory by sundown, however, so before dark we pulled up stakes, counted heads, and began to make our way back toward the canal. But first, we had to spend a day in Portobelo.

Crew Leavings

Portobelo was an amazing place, incredibly rich in history, and a great stop for passengers and crew alike. Portobelo had historically been the clearinghouse for the incredible wealth, the vast plundered quantities of gold and silver, flowing out of the New World back in the 1600's. What a colorful past the place had; the dread pirate Morgan controlled it for a short time, and the famous Sir Francis Drake had died and was buried there. But mostly the port changed hands back and forth between the Spanish and the English periodically, each vying for control and brutally overrunning the other on a regular basis. At one point, the Spanish had held it long enough that, in addition to the elaborate forts they built, they added a church and a nunnery. The next time the English invaded, they first overran the nunnery, then used the nuns as shields as they advanced upon the fort, thinking the Spanish probably would hesitate to shoot the nuns, but, of course, it didn't work, the Spanish soldiers probably having gone to Catholic schools. Times were rough back then; the whole concept of human rights violations apparently hadn't been invented yet.

The surviving ruins of the forts were incredible. Rusting cannons were still in the bulwarks, and old Spanish coins still turned up underfoot regularly. It is now designated a World Heritage Site, but, back then, it was wide open, just moldering ruins in the jungle, and no one to supervise comings and goings, a great place to wander around.

The village of Portobelo also held some charms for the crew, primarily a little ramshackle bar built out over the water with cheap beer and an old jukebox full of obscure music, and, since the ship spent the night there at anchor, there was the never-to-be-missed opportunity for the crew to take some shore leave after the dinner cleanup and chores were done.

It was probably the rampant holiday spirit and general craziness infecting the whole group that prompted Viveka, one of our young stewards, to venture out with the rest of the crew that night. She was a great kid, a sweet and earnest girl who had immediately charmed everyone and become a favorite. But she was so timid you could hardly get a word out of her, much less talk her into venturing out on these shore leave shenanigans. That's why everybody was so pleased when she decided to come along. And maybe why she was never without a fresh beer in front of her at the bar when everybody got settled in. It seemed like she was finally overcoming her shyness and was starting to unwind.

Now one of the unusual features of this particular bar was the restroom arrangement. It was a little shack at the end of a long boardwalk leading out over the water, with just a hole in a board where the toilet would be, but an imminently workable arrangement since the tide flowed in and out, a natural flushing mechanism.

Mostly, people didn't pay any further attention to the arrangement after the first time they used it, and the novelty wore off. But, Viveka hadn't been here before and seemed reluctant to make the trip, even though it was becoming apparent that she was in some discomfort from the numerous beers she'd had. But, finally, there was no putting it off any longer, and she surreptitiously slipped away when she thought no one was looking and made her way out to the shack.

I don't know how or why these kinds of things always happen just when they are least welcome, it's uncanny, but for some reason just when she was getting started, all other sound in the bar ceased. The jukebox stopped and there was a momentary lull in every conversation at every table in the entire place. The bar was almost full, too, packed with locals as well as our crew. Suddenly, there was nothing but a sound like a fire hose splashing into the water, and all eyes turned toward the shack. It went on for an inordinate, unbelievable length of time and then some more. No one spoke; everyone was transfixed, silent in appreciation. When it finally sputtered to a stop and Viveka appeared, it was to a rousing ovation, everyone on their feet and clapping and whistling, a very appreciative crowd. Beet red doesn't describe the color that came to her face, maybe fire engine red. You could tell she was trying as hard as she could to disappear, and it was some time before she let anyone talk her into venturing out again.

A Transitory Sulk

The Panama Canal pilots were required to ride aboard our ship when we went through the canal, but word had spread that we didn't need any assistance, and that there was a full bar aboard with unlimited complimentary Bloody Marys, so the usual routine was for the pilot to come aboard, check in, and then retire to the lounge, which is exactly what happened that next morning.

We had gotten permission to use the side tie arrangement in the locks, which meant that we just drove ourselves from lock to lock and tied off to the floating bollard in the lock wall. The technique the designated driver used was to get the ship all lined out headed straight into the lock, and then switch control over and quickly run to the outside wing station controls at the side of the bridge to maneuver to the wall. It was a little nerve-racking, but of course doubly so for Little, wound tight as he was. There was no excuse for Tugboat to have done what he did, but again, it may have been the general craziness that seemed to be affecting the whole ship that week.

Little was on watch as we entered the first lock, and all was going along nicely. But, unbeknownst to anyone else, Tugboat had sneaked out and locked the door leading to the wing station from the outside as a prank, and was standing by the controls out there, ready to take over when Little switched over. His plan worked perfectly, misguided as it was. Little hit the door at full stride and started scrabbling at the dogged door in complete panic; you could actually see scratch marks in the paint later. Tugboat calmly brought the boat alongside, chuckling evilly; he really got too much pleasure out of torturing his fellow mate. But the plan backfired this time. Little was so incensed that he went to his stateroom and stayed there the entire rest of the day, and Tugboat had to cover for him. He had gone too far this time; I was on Little's side on this one; that kind of behavior just wouldn't do. He was running a risk of getting smitten by lightning, or turned into salt, or

210

something, judging by what I was told later when I finally heard about it.

Flower Power Island

The passengers were enjoying their canal transit. We rose up through the three locks on the Atlantic side and started across. It was a beautiful day in Gatun Lake, with monkeys and parrots in the trees on Barro Colorado Island and little alligator-like caimans slipping into the water from the reeds as we passed. The hotel staff had ill advisedly (for this group anyway), set up a no-host bar on the upper deck, and it was immediately availed upon, and the crowd grew a bit raucous as the day wore on.

Everyone was in fine form when we locked down that afternoon on the Pacific side and made our way out to the Pearl Islands to dock at Taboga Island for a little stroll before dinner.

Now, Taboga is a little gem of an island, with narrow streets and walkways. No cars are allowed on the island, the streets are too narrow anyway, and a profusion of flowers cascades from every balcony, prompting the local nickname "Isle of Flowers." It is altogether a charming and accommodating island, a perfect place for a leisurely stroll and quiet reflection, just what I thought this group could use at this point.

It seemed to be working, various groups and couples were walking the quiet streets, and things were settling down nicely. It came time for everyone to return to the ship, and I noticed one of the last to board was my stocky cigar-chomping friend from the bridge visit seemingly starting up a conversation with one of the ubiquitous soldiers, teenagers with machine guns, who patrol every dock and public area in Panama. What was unusual was that I knew this soldier from previous trips, a friendly young kid, but one I knew didn't speak any English, so I was a bit surprised to see our passenger chatting away, in what I assumed to be Spanish, and I leaned over the bridge rail to eavesdrop.

It turned out to be English he was speaking, and what I heard of the one-sided conversation was this:

"I oughta take that gun and stick it up your ass," was what my new acquaintance was saying to the young soldier, who was nodding and smiling in non-comprehension. This wouldn't do. I quickly called down an all-aboard, cutting the conversation short, and sent the soldier a friendly wave, which he returned with a smile. I had to wonder about the lack of the instinct for self-preservation that some people exhibit when abroad. Do they act that way at home? Most of these soldiers here spoke at least some English, and that would have been awkward. We got out of there and headed south, down to the jungle where we would be safe.

Tough act to follow...

We were in the habit of stopping at one of the little fishing villages peopled by descendants of West African slaves on the outskirts of the Darien on our way down there, mainly to illustrate the diversity of peoples living side-by-side in this area, as a contrast to the Choco Indians we were going to visit. We would normally do a quick stop, in exchange for a hefty landing fee, at a little village called Punta Alegre (Happy Point), not really an apt name for this flyblown little outpost, but it had a nice ring to it.

Antonio would normally lead our group through the village, checking out the fishing net repair area and some other points of interest, and talk with a few of the inhabitants, and that would usually be the extent of it.

This visit was different, of course, just like the rest of this trip. The group came reeling back to the ship early and looked to be in some kind of shock, horrified expressions on their faces and Antonio babbling incoherently; it took some time before we could sort out what had happened.

It seemed Antonio had gathered everyone together in the center of the village and was in the process of explaining the history of the area, when he noticed he was gradually losing his audience; people were slipping away behind a shack off the main road. The crowd finally thinned to such a degree that he was forced to abandon his talk and join the other group, and he arrived there at just the pivotal moment.

A little yellow dog had been staked out spread-eagled on a board...no one could figure out why. The crowd was just watching until a huge guy with a machete appeared and quickly whacked off the dog's testicles, resulting of course in unearthly shrieking and howling, mostly coming from the dog, but probably some of it coming from our passengers as well. It was simply an animal control procedure, but it was the unexpected nature of the surgery that I think was the problem.

Anyway it pretty much ruined lunch; we didn't see the bird-watching ladies for the rest of the day.

Breakdown

It was about this time that the water maker quit, not a big surprise of course, considering the way everything else was going. We figured we'd be okay, though, since we only had a couple more days to go and the tanks were full. We would need to start rationing water, however, starting with asking people to cut back on showering. We were starting to have some problems with the air conditioning as well; the engineers suspected

213

a coolant leak somewhere; it just wasn't working like it should.

We made our way up the Tuira River to the mouth of the Mogue River, at the end of which our village was located, and anchored to await the morning high tide. We had to time the trip with the shore boats up and back at high tide because the river turned into a mud wallow at low tide, and we certainly didn't want to be stuck up there when that happened.

We had the little boats in the water at sunrise; it looked like a perfect day for a jungle adventure. Mate Little was going along on this excursion, we usually had at least one officer along on expeditions like this, and in addition to his usual gear he was carrying a large plastic bag filled with what looked like clothing. When I asked him what was in the bag, he replied gifts for the natives, but when I had a closer look it was composed entirely of brassieres of all sizes and colors. Offended by the nakedness of the Choco women, in his religious zeal, he had taken it upon himself to clothe their nakedness; he had bought out an entire department store worth of bras back in Panama City. Unbelievable. I can't even imagine what a sight that would have been if he had succeeded in delivering his gifts. All those tattooed Choco women, from young girls to old ladies, wearing loincloths and done up in bras of all sizes and colors, the mind boggles. I relieved him of the bag, with a little speech about that kind of thing not being our job here, and thanked whatever lucky stars had allowed me to catch his moral improvement scheme in time. These guys were wearing me out.

Silent Night

The passengers headed up the river for their visit, while we tried in vain to get the ship's air conditioning

214

back into shape. Unfortunately, all we succeeded in doing was breaking it down altogether. This wasn't good; tonight was not only the Captain's Farewell Dinner, but also Christmas Eve, and it was exceedingly hot and humid here in the jungle.

In keeping with everything else that had gone awry on this star-crossed trip, some of the passengers were so slow in leaving the village (apparently some rare birds had been sighted and a chase ensued), that they almost missed the tide coming out, and some of the group had to get out and push, shades of Humphrey Bogart in *The African Queen.* It was a very hot and muddy group who returned to a hot and water rationed ship. Open Bar Time.

Somehow we made it through the festivities, liberal amounts of champagne easing the struggle. It was one of the longest dinners of my life, and most of it belongs in the repressed-memory file.

At the end of it, the exhausted crew were sitting in the now empty dining room, a glazed expression on their faces, most of the passengers having retired to the lounge or the cooler outer decks. A plan was formed. It was Christmas Eve, after all, and the crew had performed brilliantly in difficult circumstances, and everybody was a long way away from home. It was suggested that we all retire to the walk-in freezer for some hot-buttered rum and Christmas carols, and that is exactly what we did. The passengers would have to fend for themselves for a little while. Someone brought down a tiny Christmas tree that we placed on top of the frozen meat locker. Mugs were filled with hot drinks. With breath steaming in the frozen air, we sang every carol we knew. As I looked around at our little group huddled around our tree, I realized that I had become very fond of these people in a short time; we had been through some trying times together, and we had formed bonds that would probably last a lifetime. It was turning out to be a pretty good trip after all.

Life in a Northern Town

Arctic Dreaming

My old shipmate and partner in crime Dippold and I eventually started a travel consulting company called Small Planet Adventures, thinking we might be able to put our combined dissolute travel experience to some use planning and putting together trips for others in some out of the way places.

We would occasionally get calls for help from some of the larger operators when they were heading into unknown territories, and we of course would take anything that came our way and sort out the details later.

One early request came in from an upscale cruise line operator who was promoting an Arctic Odyssey on a small cruise ship, offering a Russian and American arctic voyage and they wanted some help in offering some unusual destinations, with a global warming perspective. They were keen on visiting, among other destinations, Shishmaref Island, which had been in the news recently as experiencing pronounced effects of melting permafrost. Pictures of houses tumbling into the sea there had recently been on television and it had become a sort of poster child for the graphic effects of climate change. Of course we could help, this sounded fascinating.

For the Russian portion they had already engaged a Russian company familiar with the complexities of travel there, so we were tasked with helping to set up the US side of the trip.

We started to string together a logical progression of site visits, poring over charts and making endless phone calls to old contacts and village community leaders exploring the possibilities of cruise ship visits to various northern sites.

During our initial investigations we were pleased to discover that their target village of Shishmaref seemed eager for visitors, (the prospect of tourism is not always welcome in remote areas). Displays of native art and life were discussed over staticky radiophone connections with village leaders, along with discussions of some community dancing performances and village tours. Shishmaref had not done anything like this before, but the idea was discussed at local public meetings there and the consensus came back that they would welcome our guests. Fees were arranged, and landing and anchor sites were identified. They assured us there was a couple of good beach landing areas and anchorages for the ship.

But as for anchoring there, it was troubling that in our discussions with boat captains we talked to who had recently been near the area, and in looking at our satellite photos, it seemed water depth might be a problem around the island, despite the villagers' assurances to the contrary and inconclusive old chart data. We knew a site visit to these destinations was imperative. But for the moment we sketched in the Shishmaref visit as a go and rounded out our trip plan.

Time was getting short, the cruise company needed to get a firm itinerary printed into their brochure soon, so I started booking my travel and flights to our destinations to finalize the plans.

No Place Like...

I figured that the infamous town of Nome, the end of the Iditarod trail, would be a logical centralized home base from which to make forays out to the various target sites, and I eagerly headed off.

Now for all of us who harbor romantic notions about many of the places on the planet we have heard tales of and fantasized about all of our lives, places made famous by books and films and stories, there is bound to be some disappointment when reality collides with our imaginations. Varying degrees of disappointment are likely, and there is always some adjustment toward a more quotidian view of these fanciful places of our minds when confronted with the real deal. And Nome was no exception. I blame (unfairly to be sure), the Walt Disney and similar types of idealized cartoon world-views we were exposed to as kids to for this romantic phenomenon in our generation. I still want the world to be that way and am invariably saddened when it isn't.

Anyway I really did know better. I knew the quaint snow-covered dog-sled-connected village full of friendly fur-parka-wearing denizens of my mind didn't really exist, and the depressing collection of shabby structures and Quonset huts leaning against each other in the mud I found when I arrived there was really no surprise. But in compensation, the famous Nome did possess an inordinate number of bars. When I walked down the main street almost every other doorway led into a smoky view of neon over a pool table, boozy laughter and loud music bouncing off the worn

219

floorboards, serious drinking places complete with the odd inert plaid-shirted body passed out under a table or on the boardwalk outside. I would check out some of these comfortable dens later, but for now I didn't relish the idea of actually living next to or on top of one of these fragrant noisy places, where most of the rooms for rent were located. I had work to do, and I needed a quiet home base and a place to store my stuff.

I was very fortunate to find soon after arriving a tidy little bed and breakfast on the outskirts of town run by a transplanted young Californian woman and her daughter who had moved to Nome looking for a fresh start and a new outlook, and it was perfect; a warm friendly home. It was like visiting the house of an old friend, an island of order and calm amidst the relative squalor. It even had a white picket fence. I again thanked whatever saint or northern deity it was who looked out for travelers and fools, and I gratefully booked myself in for a couple of weeks and settled in and began to make my plans.

My first order of business was to visit Shishmaref, that was really the biggest unknown. Most of our other destinations, such as St. Lawrence Island, St. Paul, Shumagin and Simidi Islands, I had either been to or had first hand accounts from many of my old colleagues who had been there. But Shishmaref was unknown territory, and despite the assurances I had been given earlier, I was feeling a bit anxious to actually get out there and see for myself if we could deliver on our promises.

There were a few challenges. One immediate problem was that there was no commercial lodging available out there; it wasn't a place set up for casual visitors obviously. But after some lengthy communications it was arranged that I could possibly stay in the local parsonage with the pastor and his wife, the only other non-native people living in the village, and after some communications with the church leaders, and a donation fee agreed upon, the deal was arranged.

I caught one of the irregularly scheduled flights from Nome to Shishmaref, the little plane stuffed with locals and their gear and purchases. I was obviously out of place in the group. I was eager to engage with my taciturn fellow passengers and introduce myself, but the noise in those little planes prevents any real communication, so we just exchanged polite nods and smiles as I was covertly scrutinized, a feeling that never left me on these trips. I was reminded of having once seen on a friend's farm an unfortunate duckling who had who had somehow mistakenly imprinted upon a hen with her brood of chicks instead of his duck mother, following along with her group never realizing from his perspective that he was different, and probably wondering why the other chicks were looking at him so strangely, he thought he fit in.

After landing on the little dirt strip on the edge of Shishmaref everyone gathered up their things and we all walked the quarter-mile or so into the village and I had a chance to talk with some of these residents. It seemed that everyone knew of the upcoming impending possible ship visit, but I got the impression that the community was somewhat divided on the prospect. And honestly I could see their point. There was of course the obvious financial reward of the visits, everyone knew people in other communities who were benefitting from the new wave of tourism.

But the residents weren't oblivious to the dangers imposed by this intrusion into their traditional way of

221

life. It is a common mistake to judge a rural indigenous people as unsophisticated, as they often have as astute or better grasp of their place in the larger picture as the smug outsider. One of the most insightful discussions I have ever had about cultural upheaval and its dangers was a thoughtful talk I'd had the previous year with a wise Yu'pik man in Gambell on St. Lawrence Island when I had visited there. He had just gotten back home after a trip to Nome and had spent his last night there in the drunk tank and was in a reflective mood. In his opinion our global warming problem was a sort of fever produced by the land trying to rid itself of the sickness that was us, we greedy people who dispensed evil poison and took indiscriminately with no respect or thought for conservation of the land, tradition, or proper behavior.

Shishmaref itself had always been wary of outside influences, illustrated by the fact that they had always voted themselves a dry community, having seen the effects of alcohol on some of their neighboring islands. There had apparently been some heated community meetings on the possibility of a ship visit, but in the end it was decided the advantages outweighed the risks. The outside world had found them, as evidenced by the film crews who had recently visited to document the melting shorelines, and things were changing.

Separation of Church and Mental State

Once in the village I made my way to the church to meet my hosts, and although grateful for their hospitality and the kindness of strangers, I have to say the experience from the beginning was kind of...weird. The parsonage was a little frame house next to the church, but it looked deserted. All of the windows were covered by drawn shades and it had a neglected abandoned feel. But when I tentatively knocked on the

222

door it was cautiously opened by the parson's wife, and she didn't look...balanced I guess is the word, although I couldn't put my finger on what exactly gave me that impression. In any case she seemed uncomfortable, and I tried to put her at ease as she showed me my room and explained the rules of the common bathroom, the only flush toilet on the island, she said. I could use it but it was only to be flushed once a day, as they had to carry water for the tank. I was beginning to appreciate her haunted look. I never did see the shades opened on the windows, and I'm certain she rarely if ever set foot outside. I had the impression she desperately regretted following her husband, a dedicated sincere religious man, to this perceived savage place and was wildly eager to escape, but that could have been my imagination. (As could have been the impression that she was awkwardly coming on to me one night after dinner, I choose to believe that was just my imagination anyway. Weepers. I know my moral compass is in occasional need of minor adjustment, but this was too much.) At any rate it was uncomfortable and odd, and I hope that young ministerial couple eventually moved on to some place more suitable for them before she had a complete meltdown.

I'm Melting, melting! Oh what a world!

But as far as setting up the Shishmaref ship visit it was all coming together. I met with several village elders who had already arranged dance exhibitions and craft displays, and the row of houses that had slid and tumbled into the sea from the melting permafrost base was clearly evident at the edge of the village and was graphic testimony to changing climate conditions.

I still had to get out on the water to investigate for myself the water depth near the village however, and

I was eventually directed to an enterprising young guy who agreed to take me out in his small boat the next day. His boat didn't have a depth finder but we finally located a small handheld fathometer we could borrow from a friend of his and the outing was arranged.

We had to don waders to even get out to his boat, the fleet of village boats was anchored disconcertingly far offshore, this wasn't looking so good from the outset. As we motored further and further offshore, stopping every few minutes to take soundings, I began to have a distinct sinking feeling in the pit of my stomach. I was waiting for a drop-off, the end of the shore shelf, but it didn't appear. When we were about three miles offshore and the depth was still only around 12 feet the sinking feeling turned into a plummet. This wasn't going to work. The ship wouldn't be able to anchor anywhere close enough to shuttle passengers ashore in the skiffs, despite what we had been told, and there was certainly nowhere to dock a ship of that size. Plans and hopes had gone awry, to say the least, this was trouble and time was running out.

I had to convey my regrets to the village and made my way as quickly as possible back to Nome to regroup and come up with a new plan. And fast.

Plan B&B

I holed up in in my room back at the lodging and started plotting out an alternative replacement to that itinerary segment. After numerous frantic phone calls and frenzied chart plotting I had the outlines of a solution. Instead of Shishmaref we could stop by King Island, with its picturesque stilt village made famous by the paintings of Rie Munoz, and by the fabulous children's story and play by Jean Rogers called "A King Island Christmas", enroute to a site visit at Little

Diomede Island, a remote Island on the Russia-US border. A great solution in theory, but I still needed to do a site inspection of Little Diomede, and that wasn't going to be routine, there wasn't any regular transportation out there. It was easier in winter when the island was ice bound and they could build an airstrip on the nearby ice, but that wasn't the case now, rough seas surrounded it and there was no room for an airstrip on the rocky outcropping.

After some investigation I found out that there was a government mail helicopter that made weekly runs to the island from the nearby mainland village of Wales, and there was occasionally room for a passenger to go along on one of the runs, usually a communications maintenance man or social worker who needed to visit the island, and there was a possibility I could shoehorn myself onto one of the flights if there was an opening and I could get clearance and permission.

I happened to be at the little Nome airport when I heard this news and I immediately commandeered the public phone in the terminal to begin to make my entreaties to various government officials and postal people to try to secure a place on the helicopter that week. After innumerable calls and much wheedling on my part I was given a place in the queue, third in line after a telephone repair guy and a social worker who were already scheduled. It turned out that there was room for one passenger per trip, but as the helicopter had to make multiple trips depending upon how much mail and freight was going to the island that week, if there were enough trips required I might be able to get out there. As good a deal as I was going to find, so I signed up.

Boreal Buddy

The Nome airport terminal being a small place it was no surprise when I hung up the phone to find an attentive row of faces that had obviously been following my conversations watching me from the benches. One of the faces belonged to a little older man who immediately approached me and introduced himself. It seemed his hobby and life passion was to visit out of the way Arctic villages, and he was visibly excited. It seemed he had been doing this for some years, he was trying to visit all of the arctic villages he possibly could. I never did fully grasp his motivation, but it was his personal quest.

"You are going to Little Diomede?" he asked. "I have been trying for years to get out there, I didn't know you could ride with the mail helicopter! Do you think I could go too?"

I explained that I had just chanced upon this possibility, and it wasn't clear if there was going to be even room for me, but that he was welcome to try, and gave him the contact numbers, then went to the ticket counter to make my arrangements to fly to the staging area at Wales.

It was when I was buying my ticket to Wales that I got the first inkling that this little jaunt could turn into more of an adventure than I had bargained for. The ticket guy when he learned of my plans to fly out to Little Diomede rolled his eyes and recounted the story of one of his buddies who worked for the phone company and had done some work there the previous year. It seems weather out there was unpredictable, and his friend had made it out there fine, had done his maintenance on the tower, but then fog had rolled in and he was stuck there for twenty days waiting for it to clear.

A grim experience by his account. He said his friend always developed a slight facial tic every time he recounted the story; he didn't remember all the details, but the experience didn't sound pleasant. Yikes.

Meanwhile my new friend was ecstatic, he had secured himself the fourth position in the helicopter queue. The chances weren't good, but if there was enough freight to require four shuttle trips there was a possibility, it was just a matter of getting to the staging area and taking our chances. We were embarked on this journey together. He said he had a lot of friends in Wales and if we got out there in time there happened to be a party we could go to on Wednesday, the shuttle day, two days hence, if we got there in time.

The appointed day came, the short flight to Wales was uneventful, and it turned out we were in plenty of time to visit the party before the helicopter arrived and the shuttle flights began. We made our way to one of the scattered clapboard house that made up the village, and a full party was indeed in progress. The living room was stuffed with people; standing room only, people and relations had come from miles around. Everyone knew my new friend, he was apparently a regular visitor to the village, and we were welcomed warmly and squeezed into the fragrant throng. It was all turning a bit surreal for me. I struck up a conversation with the guy next to me; it turned out he was a whaler. Meaning he hunted whales from his little boat, harpooning them with darts attached to buoys to encumber them and keep them afloat until they could be dispatched. My God, this was living history, I was entranced. This is how his ancestors hunted whales here from prehistory, only using umiaks and air filled skin bags.

227

Plates of food were being passed around. I didn't recognize most of it, but tried everything, some delicious, some not so much to my palate, but it was fascinating. I passed a plate to the only other non-native there at the gathering besides us, a stringy biker-looking guy who had apparently married one of the local girls, but he refused, and opened his shirt to show me why. He'd had his trachea removed some years ago because of throat cancer, and the way he took sustenance was by pouring the contents of a can he carried into a small funnel in his chest, which he proceeded to do, with a great show of good humor, which didn't help my growing sense of unreality. I then struck up a conversation with woman next to me, and when she learned I was going to Little Diomede, here eyes grew large,

"I went out there last year to visit my cousin, but when the fog rolled in I was stuck for 28 days. We were scraping lichens off the rocks by the light of seal oil lamps, and when I finally got back my clothes smelled so bad I had to throw them away!" Good Lord, I was having trouble breathing in this little close room, what olfactory nightmare did she endure? Gathering lichens? I didn't have time to ask what for. To eat? I didn't want to have to do that.

It was finally time to leave to make our way to the helicopter staging area, and we bid farewell to our hosts, and I am forever grateful to have been included in that fascinating gathering, I'll never forget it.

Surly Bird

The helicopter pad was near a metal shed on the outskirts of the village, and our fellow passengers were already there waiting. The mail truck had arrived and was being unloaded, and there was quite a pile of boxes and equipment, which looked good for our chances of hitching a ride. There was also a truck containing drums of aviation fuel to refuel the helicopter between flights.

The telephone guy was there for his first foray out. I didn't think it necessary to pass along what I had heard about his predecessor getting marooned, I figured he knew what he was in for. And the young state social worker guy looked so terrified I certainly wasn't going to add to his woes. He was new at the job, he told us, and I got the impression he had drawn the short straw in this assignment, he didn't look very enthusiastic to say the least. He had a wild haunted look behind his smudged glasses, and he began to relate unbidden tales of incest and aberrant craziness, and who knew what-all, he had never been out there before either, but the social services were required to make a visit every couple of weeks. He had gotten the assignment this week and seemed woefully unready.

The chopper landed right on schedule and the pilot emerged and began loading boxes into the hold. We of course went over to try to help, but were told in no uncertain terms to go back to our waiting area, stay out of the way, and he would tell us when he was ready for one of us, one at a time and only when he told us. Wow. Not a happy guy apparently. Some of the locals joined us while we waited, and expressed their dislike for this particular pilot, not a popular fellow, and I was beginning to see their point. He was a bit prickly to say the least and probably wouldn't have made it in the tourist flightseeing game.

He and the truck driver loaded the hold and then he refueled the machine with a little gas pump from the waiting drums. When he was ready he barked for the first victim. The phone guy shuffled forward. It was like in the Wizard of Oz when Dorothy and the gang were summoned to come forward one at a time to face the Wizard, the rest of us huddling in fear and watching. He handed over an extra helmet and went through a briefing; basically sit down in the seat next to him, strap in, shut up and don't touch anything. Roger.

Off they went, the helicopter ascending with a clatter and disappearing westward. We milled about while a good portion of the village came out to watch, lots of kids roaring back and forth in the ubiquitous little ATV 4 wheel cycles that are the seasonal replacement for the winter snow machines, groups of adults were socializing, the party had moved outdoors. It was turning into quite a social event.

After about thirty minutes we could hear the helicopter returning. After landing and the loading and fueling routine was repeated, the social worker was called; the Cowardly Lion, shaking and shuffling, inched forward to meet his expected doom. He got strapped in and away they roared. Two down. To my dismay I was starting to see a wisp or two of fog developing out over the water. I kept it to myself, but it wasn't giving me a warm and fuzzy feeling. I was beginning to regret whatever it was I ate back at the house; it was doing something unruly in my stomach.

The chopper returned, the loading and fueling operations were accomplished, and it was my turn. I was brusquely given my helmet, sat down, strapped in, and we were airborne, heading quickly up and out. From this vantage point I could definitely see not just tendrils, but banks of fog forming out over the ocean. Big Diomede, the Russian island, loomed in the distance, with Little Diomede coming into view as we came closer, a helicopter landing pad becoming visible through blowing fog next to the little village clinging to the rocky mountainside. As we landed I was met by the mayor, with whom I had spoken earlier, a stocky friendly guy, and his companion, an almost freakishly tall and skinny man in native garb upon whose head perched a tall peaked wool cap, a decidedly odd looking pair. But they were accommodating and friendly and escorted me along stairways and boardwalks up the side of the mountain to the new school where the dances and presentations for our ship passengers were to take place. It looked great. There was a perfect landing place next to the helicopter pad for the ship tenders, lots of water depth for the ship, this looked like it was going to work. We made arrangements, settled on dates and a price, and the deal was pretty much done. I was feeling good about the whole affair. I wasn't feeling so good about the gathering fog however, so when I heard the helicopter returning I quickly concluded our business, bid them fond adieu, and began to make my way back to the landing pad.

The fog was really starting to settle in now and I began to hurry along the boardwalk, actually breaking into a run when I heard running footsteps behind me. It was the social worker guy. We were sprinting neck and neck in the fog. He was pretty fast. We made eye contact briefly, the whites showing all around his irises behind his fogged glasses. I am not proud of this, but I was entertaining the thought of sticking out a leg in the hopes of tripping him up. I didn't do it, but I'm ashamed to say it did cross my mind; the survival instinct is a powerful thing. I'm sure the thought occurred to him as well.

When we arrived at the landing pad who did we see emerging from the helicopter but my little friend from Nome. "Little Diomede at last!" he said. I instructed him toward the school to meet the mayor, and off he went, ecstatic. And it turned out our death sprint down the mountain hadn't been necessary after all, after the cargo was removed there were jump seats in the hold, so there was room for both of us to ride back at the same time. We exchanged high fives as we rose up from the foggy island for our trip back to Wales, giddy with relief.

When we arrived back at the staging area two things happened. First, when the pilot tried to start the little gas pump to refuel for the next trip, it flooded. He didn't have a spark plug wrench to remove the plug to dry it out, and the villagers refused to loan him one, they pretended they didn't have one, they really didn't like him. Quite some time passed before he could get the pump going, and of course the second thing that happened was that by that time the fog had settled in in earnest, so there would be no more trips that day. The realization really dawned on me as I flew away from Wales on the commercial flight, along with a healthy dose of survivor guilt; the phone guy and my new friend were in for some sort of adventure.

Oz-similation?

The trip to Little Diomede for the ship, in fact the whole northern itinerary, worked almost flawlessly, it was a great success for the cruise operator on all fronts. But I worried about the little guy I had met in Nome. I tried to call him many times, we had exchanged contact information, he had an address in New Mexico, but there was no answer. I never spoke with him again and I think of him often. I wonder if he found out why they would collect lichens by the light of seal oil lamps. He had finally made it to Little Diomede. But I can't shake the feeling that maybe he is still there. I saw some pictures from the ship visit later and in one of them a crowd of villagers is dancing the guests away at the landing site and one of them is a little guy in an odd hat that could well be him. But the picture is blurry, and he is looking down and I can't make out his face. If it was indeed my friend I hope he is happy and has finally found what he was looking for.

Captured In Black and White – A Tribute

Part One
Orca Dorky

Maui had become in the years following those early Humpback discoveries a sort of a whale Mecca for a loose group of whale researchers who made pilgrimages there as often as budgets would allow (understandably enough), which made for some lively winters in Lahaina. It was exciting to be around a group of bright young people who shared a common passion, and I felt fortunate to be a small part of it. A couple of the young grad students who came by regularly, friends of Flip Nicklin and Jim Darling's, were these two engaging guys named Graeme Ellis and John Ford who, in addition to their interest in Humpbacks, were both also involved in the developing Orca research taking place around their home territory of Vancouver Island. And when they talked about what was going on back there you couldn't help but be caught up in their enthusiasm. It sounded amazing. They said it had started a couple of years earlier almost by accident:

It seems a Canadian marine biologist named Michael Bigg had been tasked by the Department of Fisheries and Oceans Canada with the counting of local killer whales as part of a population census that was initiated after the animals had begun to be captured in increasing numbers for marine parks and aquariums. Apparently, a population count was standard procedure in situations like this. Although it was assumed that there were thousands of these whales swimming around the area (so theoretically grabbing up a few here and there wouldn't impact the population much), they needed to make sure before they designated them "harvestable" and declared open season. And it would have been quite the open season, too, since each successfully captured orca was worth tens of thousands of dollars at that time on the open market.

But not only did Michael Bigg discover that the number of local resident whales was actually drastically lower than previously thought, only numbering in the several hundreds instead of the several thousands (numbers so low as to threaten their sustainability), he also, in spending time with them, came to realize something else. These whales were incredibly enmeshed in a complex and fascinating social web that could only be described as a cetacean society, and in his opinion desperately needed to be protected and studied.

Now governments are not known for their far-reaching scientific curiosity in matters that don't impact or threaten them directly or immediately, and DFO Canada was no exception in this case. The population count Michael Bigg had been instructed to collect was received and assessed, a determination was correctly made to prohibit further captures, and Michael Bigg was assigned something else to count, and ordinarily that

235

would have been the end to it. But, fortunately, Michael Bigg was not ordinary.

He was hooked. He continued to study and document these killer whale pods, even when there was no longer a program or funding available for that purpose, sometimes gathering photo IDs and data in the course of ostensibly studying something else, sea lions or seals, or sometimes just on his own at his own expense in his little boat. And what he was finding out was becoming more fascinating on an almost daily basis.

He was developing and refining his photo identification system. He had quickly discovered that each individual whale had his or her own unique saddle patch pattern (the light-colored area at the base of the dorsal fin), enabling him to begin to recognize individuals and to start to understand family groupings and relationships. And there was a lot going on.

Family groups were straightforward, no big surprises there. (Except maybe the fact that the males stayed with their mothers all of their lives, big mama's boys, like those gigantic professional football players who always cry in television interviews when they talk about their mamas.) But what he found especially interesting was the variety and interrelationships of subgroups, and the additional element involving vocalizations, the sounds he could hear when he dropped a hydrophone in the water when he was drifting around near them. Several subgroups actually seemed to have their own characteristic dialect, like the difference in accents between someone from Minnesota and someone from Georgia for example; the same language but a different take on it. This was incredible stuff. He set about documenting and labeling the various groups, and assigned them letters of the alphabet to distinguish discrete groups, and then went about identifying different families within the larger groups and assigned them numbers to keep track of them; he invented the whole complex identification system that has become the standard used today. There was obviously a lot more going on here than the then-common notion of these being just a bunch of whales swimming around eating up our salmon.

This is about where Graeme and John got involved. Michael started telling anyone who would listen about this incredible world he had gotten a glimpse of, and when he showed these guys what he had been up to, they became just as hooked as he was. It was to occupy most of the rest of their respective careers.

Island Hopping

The next summer I happened to be visiting Seattle when I knew Flip was currently on nearby Vancouver Island visiting Graeme and John, so I gave him a call just to check in and say hello. Great timing as it turned out. He said that he was going to be going out with Graeme in his little boat for the next few days to help photo ID orcas, and they wondered if I would like to come along. Absolutely. I had wanted to see this ever since hearing about it in Maui. I grabbed my camera and caught the next morning's ferry to Nanaimo, an old city on the east side of Vancouver Island, to meet up with them there.

Graeme had his boat tied up in front of a quaint little English hotel outside of town, he told me, a place called the Tudor Arms or something, and we had made arrangements to all meet there for breakfast before heading out on the water.

It was a short walk from the ferry dock to the hotel, and it was quaint indeed, a proper little enclave.

237

The building itself was an imposing stone structure set in a perfect English garden setting; it was like suddenly finding yourself in a Jane Austen novel. Well-dressed reserved couples strolled along the well-tended paths. I was beginning to regret my choice of attire; worn jeans and a sweatshirt reading *"Drink 'Til You Want Me."* I felt vaguely out of place. I hadn't realized Vancouver Island would be so stuffy.

Breakfast in this place turned out to be an elaborate affair, almost an English high tea setup, including doilies, silver service, and scones and such. Flip and Graeme to their credit refrained from commenting on my outfit; they should have at least warned me what I was in for after all. In fact, the only feedback I got from anyone on my sartorial selection was a discreet arched eyebrow from the formal black-tied waiter, that's how genteel the place was.

During that interminably long (to me anyway) breakfast Graeme caught us up on some of what had been going on with the orca research they were doing. It seemed that a young orca calf from one of the local pods had been recently orphaned and was in failing health because none of the other pod members had stepped up to sponsor him, which was usually what happened in those cases. We were going to rendezvous later with Michael Bigg, who had gone out in his own boat ahead of us to see if he could locate the orphan's pod. Apparently, as Graeme explained it, when a calf's mother died, another adult would usually step in to take on the care and education of the little one, but that didn't always happen, and no one knew why. I was again struck by how complicated the relationships among these orcas were.

We headed out into a beautiful summer morning on the water, Graeme's little boat perfectly set up for the kind of photo ID work he was doing, but a little crowded for the three of us, as became evident when we soon got into some good picture taking situations. I found I couldn't get any clear shots around Flip and Graeme who, old pros that they were, immediately grabbed the good vantage points when the action started. So, I commandeered the top of the little cabin as my spot and settled in quite nicely, thank you. I was getting lots of shots I thought were good, *Dorsal Fins in the Mist* kinds of scenes; I was snapping away furiously. I normally didn't get a chance to take pictures on these excursions, and I was taking full advantage of it. I noticed Flip wasn't taking nearly as many shots as I was. When I asked him about it, he said he was waiting for better light, which surprised me; it seemed like plenty of light to me, but then I was new at this.

I may have been a bit over enthusiastic in my initial photographic salvos. I had brought along a half dozen or so rolls of film, which I thought would be more than adequate, but I was surprised when I found I was getting low, I guess I'd gotten a little excited. And then indeed the light did change; the sun broke out of the fog and obliquely illuminated the whales, the water, the bluffs in the background, spectacular. I started taking pictures in earnest. It was getting hot on top of the cabin now, so I stripped down to my gym shorts and got down to business, clicking away like mad, and then it happened. I ran totally out of film. And the day was just beginning.

Things went downhill at this point. When I asked the two miscreants down below if I could buy some film from them, I got an education on just how competitive

239

this photography business could be. Graeme refused outright; he was shooting black and white ID shots anyway. Flip allowed he was willing to sell me one roll, but for fifty dollars. He said these conditions were good, and he wasn't even sure *he* had brought enough film, and he damned sure wasn't going to risk running out by letting me burn through his film stash like he had heard me doing with mine up there earlier. Things were looking so good on the water right now, though, that I desperately needed some more film, so I accepted the fifty dollar deal and started to slide off the top to jump below to get it. That's when the world turned upside down.

Somehow when I started sliding off the top, a little metal hook on the roof's edge I hadn't noticed before just managed to catch the hem of my gym trunks and hold fast, stopping me up short in mid-air just before I touched down, leaving me suspended like a screaming piñata. My arms and legs were windmilling uncontrollably, my entire weight supported by the fabric of my shorts. It was like those pictures you see of a stork carrying an infant, but incredibly painful, as you might imagine. I don't know how long I was hanging there; Flip and Graeme were both immobilized first in surprise and then with hilarity, neither making a move to help as I swung helplessly to and fro, but mercifully the shorts finally tore through, depositing me in a heap on the deck. To this day, the memory of that scene reduces the both of them to tears of mirth, but I didn't find anything in the least amusing about it. In fact, I had just about enough of the both of them at this point, so the timing was perfect when we caught up with Michael Bigg and he asked if I wouldn't mind coming along with him in his boat to drive so he could concentrate on doing some observations. That sounded like a great idea. I was out of film anyway.

Expelled from School

Michael had indeed found the pod with the orphaned calf; we could see the youngster following forlornly a few hundred yards behind the rest of the group. It was a tragic scene.

Michael and I followed along with the calf while Graeme and Flip went ahead with the rest of the bunch. We spent most of the day observing the little guy, trying to learn as much as possible about what was going on, and Michael filled me in on what he had observed in the past in similar situations involving orphaned calves.

On one of the other occasions like this, the death of a young calf's mother, he said it had surprisingly been an uncle who had taken on the primary teaching of the youngster, but usually it would be another female, often an aunt. In these cases the older whale, whoever had taken on the sponsoring role, could be observed repeatedly catching and releasing a fish in front of the calf until it grasped the concept, and often the two would be seen to leap repeatedly from the water in tandem, for all the world as if practicing breaching lessons.

I was totally fascinated by what I was seeing, and by Michael's explanations. Things didn't look too good in this particular calf's case unfortunately. It had been several days since his mother had disappeared and he was still on his own, following forlornly behind the family, and Michael pointed out that the normally rounded area behind his blowhole, called the melon, appeared shrunken in this case, indicating that he was losing weight. It wasn't that he was too young to catch fish on his own, he was past nursing age, it was more likely that he was depressed and not eating, and it was

241

likely that he wouldn't make it. They were such social animals that they just didn't function well alone. This had a profound affect on me, on all of us and I wished there was something we could do, but of course there wasn't. Little did I know that years later I would have a chance to help when a similar situation presented itself.

Globe Trotting

After a long and memorable day on the water, we all made our way back to Nanaimo, pulling in just around dark, visions of black dorsal fins swimming before our eyes. After we secured the boats and equipment and bid our goodbyes to Michael, who was catching a ferry back to the mainland, Graeme announced that he had the perfect spot in mind for dinner. Since all we'd eaten since that scone-filled breakfast were a couple of the world's oldest and driest granola bars, we set off. We needed some cheering up, Graeme said, after the sad experience with the orphaned calf and this would be just the ticket. The place we were going, a bar and grill called *The Globe*, was an institution, he told us, not only a great place to eat but incidentally also the premier strip club on all of Vancouver Island, and not to be missed.

He was right. We got a great table up near the front (like our teachers told us, "*You have to sit up near the front of the class if you want to learn anything…*"), ordered some drinks and dinner, and settled in for the spectacle. The food was fantastic, and we were making the acquaintance of dancer #2; she was far and away our favorite, and I'm sure she liked us, too; she seemed to be paying us special attention. It was after dessert that one of us had a visit from that Good Idea Fairy; the Good Idea in this case being that it would be fun to join #2 in a dance onstage, and of course hilarity ensued. It all

242

ended up with us being escorted out of the place by some nice large people; everybody seemed so polite up here. All in all it was a satisfying evening, and I hadn't felt underdressed at all. We were cheered up, just as Graeme had promised. Vancouver Island wasn't that stuffy a place after all.

But the memory of that day with Michael Bigg and I following that doomed lonesome young whale stayed with me.

Part Two
Spring Forward

Many years later, I was to be acutely reminded of that day when word came that a lone orca calf had shown up hanging around a public ferry dock in Seattle. It was strange, the calf was obviously too young to be on its own. Stranger still, its markings and vocalizations seemed to identify it as a northern resident, one of those same northern Vancouver Island whales we had followed so long ago. But it was a long way from home; those northern residents were not known to travel much farther south than Nanaimo, and this whale was a couple of hundred miles from there.

It was a mystery, and the experts were called in. The experts in this case were now Graeme Ellis and John Ford.

A lot had happened in the intervening years. Michael Bigg had sadly passed away from leukemia, but not before securing his legacy. What an amazing guy. He had become recognized as a giant in the field of cetacean research, and his methods and findings are still being used today. Graeme and John had continued his work and were discovering and publishing groundbreaking stuff on a regular basis; the orcas were continuing to amaze everyone, and this new development with the wayward calf was no exception.

John had become proficient at identifying the different dialects of the various pods, and he confirmed that this was indeed a northern whale. Not only was it a northern resident, it was a whale they knew, A73, to use Michael Bigg's numbering system, a young female nicknamed *Springer*. What had happened to her mother and how she had made her way all the way down here were the subject of much speculation and anybody's guess.

The young whale obviously wasn't just passing through. She had taken up residence near the ferry dock and seemed to be attracted to the ferry, bounding out to meet it when it arrived and reluctantly following it out a ways every time it left, turning a sad eye up when she realized it was leaving. It was much like the daily performance of the beloved family dog who can't believe you would choose to spend time away from her company when you leave for the day, amazed when you leave every morning and ecstatic when you return. But it certainly wasn't normal behavior for a killer whale, and it brought about a huge amount of media attention. Flocks of people gathered on the docks to watch Springer, and film crews jostled for position on the ferry's railings. The whale needed an agent. Something had to be done. But what?

Repo Plan

The little whale was starving for the social interaction of her pod, and was endangering herself by hanging around boats and people, so, the idea of returning her to her family held enormous popular appeal, but it wasn't that simple. First of all, capturing and transporting a killer whale hundreds of miles, even a small one like Springer (but already around twelve feet long and weighing over half a ton), presented enormous logistical challenges. Then there was the problem of why she was there in the first place. Just as Michael Bigg had observed to me all those years ago, sometimes nature operates in ways not readily apparent to us; maybe there was some reason why this whale was rejected by her pod, a bad or troubled or unhealthy kid, shunned and sent away, like the black sheep remittance men sent to America from Victorian England and told never to return.

But Springer seemed healthy enough, and she clearly couldn't stay where she was. There was some brief talk of capture for an aquarium, but that met with such a public outcry that the idea was abandoned almost immediately. Options were limited.

So, reluctantly, the various groups, the governments and NGOs, and other interested parties who had a stake in this gathered quietly together to assess the feasibility of a relocation effort. The stakes were high; the specter of failure in the form of a deceased baby whale in this kind of media glare was too grim to contemplate. But how to do it? No one had ever attempted anything quite like this, there was no guarantee this could be pulled off.

An elaborate plan was formulated. Springer could be carefully captured down here, placed in a temporary net pen, tested and observed for health, then quickly transported to a similar net pen up in her home waters, then released the next time her family pod happened by. A few holes remained in the overall plan, such as how to transport a whale and what might happen if her family wasn't so happy to see her again when she was released, but it was a plan nonetheless.

Capturing the calf could be done; similar things had been done before, and there was a perfect National Marine Fisheries research net pen already in place near the ferry dock at the Seattle end. Researcher Paul Spong volunteered his research facility on the north side of Vancouver Island as a location for the receiving pen, so far so good. A medical and handler team was put into place, the Vancouver Aquarium taking the lead on this, with some trainers coming aboard from various marine parks, all in all an impressive group. Transport was still a problem, however. The common wisdom was that the calf could be transported in a large tank (whales can't survive long without being suspended in water), but not for more than a limited number of hours, ten or twelve at the most, and the trip was around 350 miles between pens. An aircraft delivery was proposed, but then abandoned as impractical and prohibitively expensive.

Transport was the only remaining piece of the puzzle. This was where my old friends at Nichols Brothers Boat Builders came in and how I got involved.

The Good Idea Ferry

As luck would have it (for this project anyway, not necessarily for Nichols), one of the large passenger ferries the shipyard had recently built for a foreign client had been repossessed for lack of payment and had been sitting idle for several months at their yard on Whidbey Island while the bank sorted things out; it could be made available for this transport. These were fast boats, forty knots, and big, with seats for 400 passengers or so, and with a large back deck that could accommodate a tank with a whale in it. In a spontaneous gesture of altruistic public service, the company volunteered the boat, along with me to help drive it, for the project. It was perfect. We could get Springer aboard and be up at Paul Spong's

246

place in ten hours if all went according to plan; now, we just needed to sort out the details. This was going to be fun.

Now that the pieces were in place things began to move quickly. We didn't have much time to get the ship out of mothballs and into service. Fuel was trucked in, engines were started, systems were checked, oil was changed, and the big tank for Springer's Big Adventure was installed on the back deck, complete with a makeshift piped-in water supply system so sea water could be pumped through continually, like a big version of a home aquarium. I gathered up charts and gear and we prepared for the trip.

This was turning into a big event. Not only was there constant media attention, the shipyard had also invited fifty or so friends and family along for the ride, so things were becoming hectic. We were scheduled to leave the next morning at dawn to travel the few miles from Whidbey Island down to the pen where Springer was. A big crane was waiting to lift her into the tank, and off we would go.

Sunrise found a huge crowd down at the boat, families with coolers and blankets and cameras swarmed aboard; it looked like a crowded morning at the beach, everybody piling in and setting up camp. The main deck was open to guests, shipyard families, and other passersby and the second deck was reserved for media and government officials and other elite. Sort of like the Titanic, with steerage down below and first class and VIPs above; kind of odd, but I guess predictable. I had brought my wife Cherie along, and we watched in awe from the bridge as this all unfolded beneath us. She went below momentarily and almost didn't make it back up; a minor Aquarium official had set herself up as the arbiter of upper deck passage, like the doorman at an exclusive nightclub, and Cherie had to do some fast talking to gain access to the rarified air of the second deck.

We got everyone aboard, cast off the lines, and headed out. All seemed well until we tried to come up to speed, and it just didn't happen. The boat had been sitting idle for so long that barnacles and other marine growth had settled in and clogged the water jets. We weren't even making twenty knots, much less the thirty-five or so we needed to average to get Springer up to her home waters in the allotted time. This was embarrassing. We needed to get some divers down to clean away the offending stuff, and that would take some time, so back to the dock we went. We were certain we didn't want to continue down to Springer's pen with this news, where a full-blown media circus was taking place, with huge crowds and klieg lights and helicopters. We were feeling foolish enough without subjecting ourselves to that kind of thing; there would likely be some pointed questions along the lines of why we hadn't done some sort of speed trial, and we didn't have a satisfactory answer.

We got tied back up and quickly got a team of divers working on clearing the jets, but we had missed our window of opportunity timing-wise; Springer's trip would have to wait until the following day.

The next morning was much like the previous one, but the crowd at our dock had thinned somewhat, thankfully as it turned out. It was grueling enough with the numbers we ended up with.

We made it down to the pen as scheduled this time, and the craning operation went flawlessly. The little calf seemed non-plussed about the whole operation, suspended serenely in her sling as she was moved over to the tank on the ship. Of course, the tranquilizers probably helped some. It wasn't long before I wished they could have administered some of those drugs to a few of the whale's handlers as well.

Along with Springer, we gained a team of vets and whale trainer folks, who were great, and some Aquarium and Department of Fisheries Canada officials, who were not. Some guy named John Blackbird from the Aquarium started screaming that he was in control of all media and that no one was to take any photos without his permission and that he wanted the ships internal video system turned off so no one could sneak pictures of that. Then, some DFO bigwig, Madeline something, made herself objectionable by establishing herself in the bridge and issuing all manner of directives. I understood that they were all worked up by this project, but a little talk about shipboard procedure seemed to be in order at this point. I had to explain that they weren't in charge when aboard, sadly enough for them, and the ship's video system would remain on for safety reasons. And whatever directives they felt moved to issue needed to be cleared through the captain first. It wasn't a happy beginning, but I was feeling a bit on edge myself. It might have had something to do with all of those bright lights.

We got settled in to our tense standoff and got underway. Actually it felt pretty good. We had a camera trained on the whale tank we could watch from the bridge, and Springer looked happy floating there in her tank. I had the first faint glimmering that maybe we could pull this off after all, but we still had a long way to go.

Madeline began asking every few minutes when we were going to cross the border into Canada. The tenth time she asked, I had to ask her what exactly was going to happen when we crossed…was she going to imagine herself even *more* empowered? I regretted asking it immediately; she didn't seem to take it well.

Positively Reinforced

All was initially going along well, but a couple of hours into the trip we started to experience some alarm problems with one of the engines; nothing wrong with the engine, just a faulty alarm. Every ten minutes or so, the alarm buzzer would scream into life and require someone to hit the silence button on the engineer's console. It was more annoying than anything else, once we knew what it was. On top of that, we were burning more fuel than we had calculated, probably due to the jets still having some growth in them that the divers hadn't been able to get to.

The alarm problem was taken care of in short order. The engineer was a big friendly hulking guy from the shipyard I had known for years named Downer. He was hunkered down in the big chair at the engineer's station, and I had stationed a deckhand next to him with a can of peanuts. Every time the alarm sounded, he hit the button, and the deckhand would pop a peanut into his mouth. It was a great system, and it worked flawlessly. Downer was doing a wonderful job, and he looked pleased; I knew he loved peanuts.

The fuel consumption was another matter, however. At the rate we were going through it, we weren't going to be able to make it all the way to Paul's place. That would *really* be embarrassing, coasting to a stop in full view of the national news media, worse than running out of gas on a crowded freeway. We decided we would have to do a pit stop in a little town called Campbell River about halfway there.

It turned out that the stop was going to work out perfectly anyway. Springer was starting to overheat, and the vets asked us if there was anywhere we could stop and get some ice. So, we called ahead to the fuel dock and ordered a hundred or so bags of ice, and we ordered a few dozen pizzas while we were at it.

It was odd though, when we pulled into Campbell River, there was a big crowd of native First Nation people gathered there to meet us, with gifts of carved masks and potlatch items to give us, thanking us for taking Springer home. I wondered how they knew we would be stopping there; we hadn't known it ourselves until only a short time before.

The stop was perfect. We got Springer cooled off, topped off our fuel tanks, and topped everyone else off with the pizza. It was beginning to look like a refugee camp down on the main deck at this point, however, huddled bodies strewn about the floor and little tents made of blankets draped across the rows of seats. There was a faint smell of burning mattress or something; I never did find out what it was.

Offaloading

The rest of the trip went without incident. We pulled up to the waiting pen right on schedule, and there was a big crane barge waiting there to swing the cradled whale into her new temporary home. She looked positively happy hanging there, (but then I guess that is kind of the default look with orcas and other dolphins in general). Her pen had been filled with salmon donated by the local Kwakwaka'wakw native people; it must have been better than a fully stocked mini-bar at the end of a long trip.

What a sense of relief we felt. Our part of the job was complete, and I was just starting to realize how stressful this had been judging by how exhausted we all felt. Now the question on everybody's mind was what would happen when Springer was reunited with her family. We all had sudden visions of the family greeting going something along the lines of "What? You again? We thought we told you to get lost!" right before they ate her, which wouldn't play too well on the national news.

It would turn out that Springer's pod would happen by just a couple of days later, affectionate calls of greeting would ring out, and Springer would be released ultimately into the sponsorship of her grandmother, A-24, a whale nicknamed Kelsey. It would be a huge success story, almost a perfect ending to Springer's saga, but we didn't know that at the time; we were just hoping for the best.

Reunion

We limped our exhausted way over to a nearby resort village called Telegraph Cove and tied up at the dock for the night, everyone anxious to get off the boat for awhile. The emptied main deck of the ship looked like Yasgur's Farm after Woodstock, and everybody still had to spend the night and the next day aboard, realization perhaps dawning on the passengers that this little excursion was turning out to be more than they had bargained for.

Telegraph Cove is a delightful place, full of little shops and restaurants, and an old friend of ours, Jim Borrowman, operated a whale watching business out of there. Cherie and I made our way over to his place to see if he was home, and who did we find sitting there drinking wine and visiting with Jim and his wife but Graeme Ellis and John Ford. What an unexpected surprise. They were both working for DFO Canada at the time and were here for Springer's relocation.

What a great reunion. We started in on our old stories, including that day we spent with the orphaned calf with Michael Bigg years ago. I started to relate the stories of our trip up here, including the travails with the likes of John Blackbird and Madeline the Magnificent, when their eyes lit up and they said that Madeline was their boss and co-worker; in fact, she had arrived here a few minutes before we did, and was just taking a shower.

Right on cue, she walked in wearing a robe and a towel around her hair, and when she saw us sitting there visiting, wine glasses in hand, her face went through the most extraordinary transformations. It started with a blank look, then confusion; you could see the wheels moving, but nothing was connecting. I can imagine it must have been akin to seeing your pet dog suddenly stand up and begin a thoughtful conversation; something wasn't right. It was difficult to process right away. Perfunctory introductions were made, and we allowed that, yes, we had met. Jim poured her a glass of wine, and after an awkward interval, I found her to be pleasant company. As it turned out, I had occasion to work with her on several projects in the coming years, and she became a friend. It just goes to show how misleading first impressions can be.

Distant Reflections

The next morning, we hauled our bedraggled selves over to the fuel dock in Alert Bay, a native Kwakwaka'wakw village, to top off fuel and replenish our supplies. When I went below, I discovered that the main deck now looked like an overcrowded bus station in Darfur or somewhere, and smelled like someone had set a used diaper on fire. Who would *do* that? I decided to go down there as seldom as possible for the rest of the trip.

Meanwhile, Cherie had gone ashore to the store to buy some food for the trip, and there she had an unexpected profound experience. The little native woman behind the counter, upon learning that Cherie was from the boat, immediately bowed deeply, her eyes filling with tears, and said, "Thank you for bringing our Springer home to us." Obviously, the orcas still played a large part in present day native culture. It was humbling.

Fueled and restocked, we started the long trip home. As we passed by nearby Robson Bight, the little cove called the "rubbing beach" where the orcas would habitually come to roll around on the smooth stones of the bottom of the bay (and where Flip would first swim with orcas for a *National Geographic* story), I noticed that the area was now designated on the chart as the "Michael Bigg Ecological Reserve." How fitting. I gave the place a small salute as we passed by.

I thought again of that day with the little orphaned calf of long ago, and I wondered what Michael would have thought of this little adventure we had just undertaken. I think he would have been pleased.

About the Author

Michael Bennett, Small Planet Adventures owner, is at home cruising in the exotic places of the world. Over the past twenty years, he has piloted boats for many *National Geographic* magazine and film expeditions. An ardent diver and skilled Captain, Michael teamed with world-renowned photographer Flip Nicklin in Patagonia, Panama, Brazil, Hawaii, Sri Lanka, Canada, and Costa Rica to document whales, dolphins, and other exotics.

Prior to launching Small Planet, Michael was an Expedition Cruise Ship Captain, steering vessels through nearly every corner of the globe. He then went on to launch one of the first successful luxury yacht cruising companies. A fervent advocate for whales, Michael is past president of the Whale Watch Operators Association, and has helped develop the guidelines for responsible whale watching presently in use today. He was also one of the captains who drove Springer the orphaned Orca from the US back to her home in Canada.

His enthusiasm and respect for the wonderful places and experiences on our planet is infectious, and he is happiest when he is sharing them.

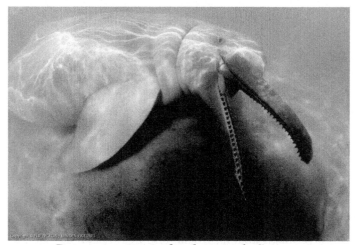

Boto swooping in for the attack. Scary...

Tucuxi love attack! Creepy...

Sri Lanka. Definitely not in Kansas anymore…

But wearing the proper helmet.

Sailing away in Patagonia.

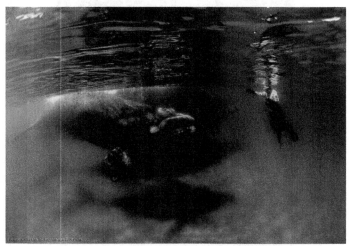

Between a mother and her calf... hmm...

Running the Rogue.

Cleaned up at the Back Forty.

Old Sporty with the IMAX camera on bow.

Cowboy and fish and me in front of the Pioneer Inn.

Ready or not Panama...

Christmas Eve in the Darien Jungle.

261

Bow landing in San Blas. Surprise!

Chocos wondering who we are…

Foggy landing in Diomede.

And pulling away!...yes!...

263

Springer the airborne whale.

Cherie hiding in the bridge from the Springer crowds.

Made in the USA
Middletown, DE
03 August 2021